WORKBOOK

Focus on Grammar

An **INTERMEDIATE** Course for Reference and Practice

SECOND EDITION

Marjorie Fuchs

Longman

FOCUS ON GRAMMAR: AN **INTERMEDIATE** COURSE FOR REFERENCE AND PRACTICE
Workbook

Copyright © 2000, 1994 by Addison Wesley Longman, Inc.
A Pearson Education Company.
All rights reserved.

Pearson Education, 10 Bank Street, White Plains, NY 10606

Editorial director: Allen Ascher
Executive editor: Louisa Hellegers
Director of design and production: Rhea Banker
Development editors: Angela Malovich Castro and Bill Preston
Production manager: Alana Zdinak
Managing editor: Linda Moser
Senior production editor: Virginia Bernard
Production editor: Christine Lauricella
Senior manufacturing manager: Patrice Fraccio
Manufacturing manager: David Dickey
Cover design: Rhea Banker
Text design adaptation: Rainbow Graphics
Text composition: Rainbow Graphics
Photo credits: **p. 4** Rubberball Productions; **p. 14** AP/Wide World Photos; **p. 15** Library of Congress; **p. 17** AP/Wide World Photos; **p. 54** AP/Wide World Photos; **p. 74** Allsport Photography (USA), Inc; **p. 74** AP/Wide World Photos; **p. 87** Rubberball Productions; **p. 91** Hulton Getty; **p. 102** Ken Biggs/Tony Stone Images; **p. 102** Tony Stone Images; **p. 131** Rubberball Productions

0–201–34679–6

3 4 5 6 7 8 9 10—BAH—04 03 02 01 00

CONTENTS

iii

ABOUT THE AUTHOR

Marjorie Fuchs has taught ESL at New York City Technical College and LaGuardia Community College of the City University of New York and EFL at the Sprach Studio Lingua Nova in Munich, Germany. She holds a Master's Degree in Applied English Linguistics and a certificate in TESOL from the University of Wisconsin–Madison. She has authored or co-authored many widely used ESL textbooks, notably *On Your Way: Building Basic Skills in English, Crossroads, Top Twenty ESL Word Games, Around the World: Pictures for Practice, Families: Ten Card Games for Language Learners, Focus on Grammar: A High-Intermediate Course for Reference and Practice*, and the *Workbooks* to the *Longman Dictionary of American English*, the *Longman Photo Dictionary, The Oxford Picture Dictionary,* and the *Vistas* series.

UNIT

1

PRESENT PROGRESSIVE AND SIMPLE PRESENT TENSE

❶ SPELLING

Add **-ing** *to these verbs to form the present participle. Add* **-s** *or* **-es** *to form the third-person-singular form. Make spelling changes where necessary.*

	-ing	-s or -es
1. start	starting	starts
2. get	_____	_____
3. try	_____	_____
4. plan	_____	_____
5. have	_____	_____
6. do	_____	_____
7. match	_____	_____
8. grab	_____	_____
9. give	_____	_____
10. say	_____	_____

❷ SIMPLE PRESENT TENSE OR PRESENT PROGRESSIVE

Complete the sentences about a student, Antonio Lopes. Use the correct form of the verbs in parentheses ( ).

1. It's 8:00 A.M. Antonio Lopes _____ is driving _____ to school.
   (drive)

2. He _____ to school every day.
   (drive)

3. The trip usually _____ 25 minutes.
   (take)

4. Today it _____ 25 minutes.
   (not take)

5. It _____ much longer.
   (take)

(continued on next page)

6. Workers _____ the highway this morning.
   (repair)

7. Because of the construction, Antonio _____ Parson Road.
   (use)

8. He _____ usually _____ Parson
   (not use)
   Road.

9. Normally, he _____ Route 93.
   (take)

10. Traffic always _____ faster on Route 93.
    (move)

11. Today, the weather _____ the traffic, too.
    (slow down)

12. It _____ hard, and the roads are slippery.
    (rain)

13. Antonio _____ to drive in the rain.
    (not like)

14. Antonio's a careful driver, and he always _____ slowly
    (drive)
    when the roads are wet.

15. The radio is on, and Antonio _____ to the traffic report.
    (listen)

16. He always _____ to the radio on his way to work.
    (listen)

17. The announcer _____ an accident on Parson Road.
    (describe)

18. Antonio _____ to be late for school, but there's nothing he
    (not want)
    can do.

19. Traffic _____ because of the accident.
    (not move)

20. Antonio _____ to drive when the traffic is bad.
    (hate)

21. He never _____ relaxed when he is behind the wheel.
    (feel)

22. He _____ he can't do anything about the traffic conditions.
    (know)

23. Antonio _____ he were on the bus instead.
    (wish)

3 PERSONALIZATION

_Complete these statements with information about yourself. Use the
present progressive or the simple present tense._

1. At the moment _____.

2. I always _____.

3. I sometimes _____, but now I _____.

4 PRESENT PROGRESSIVE OR SIMPLE PRESENT TENSE

*Read and complete these postcards with the present progressive or
simple present tense form of the verbs in the boxes.*

| blow | build | feel | fly | know | shine | ~~sit~~ |

1.

Dear Megan,

Hi! I _____'m sitting_____ on the beach at Ipanema. The weather is beautiful.
_____1._____

The sun _____, and there isn't a cloud in the sky. A soft breeze
_____2._____

_____. It _____ great.
_____3._____ _____4._____

Some beautiful tropical birds (you _____ the kind)
_____5._____

_____ above. Children _____
_____6._____ _____7._____

sand castles. This is the place to be!

Wish you were here,

Ashley

| get | have | look | stand | start | take | travel |

2.

Dear Carlos,

Ana and I _____ through England. Right now I _____ in front
_____1._____ _____2._____

of Buckingham Palace. It's a cloudy day. The sky _____ darker by the minute. It
_____3._____

_____ like it's going to rain. Ana _____ her camera, and she
_____4._____ _____5._____

_____ pictures. Oh, no! It _____ to rain.
_____6._____ _____7._____

See you in a few weeks!

Marcos

(continued on next page)

| help | improve | live | miss | speak | study | want |

3.

Dear Amanda,

Here I am in Paris! I _____ French and

                             1.

_____ with a French family—the Michauds. My French

                 2.

_____ because I always _____ it

                 3.   4.

"at home."

    The Michauds are great. They _____ me find a job.

                                     5.

I _____ to save enough money to travel in August. Why

                6.

don't you come and visit me? I _____ you!

                            7.

                                                  Melissa

5 AFFIRMATIVE STATEMENTS

Mario and Silvia are students. Look at what they do every day. Write sentences about their activities. Choose between the present progressive and the simple present tense.

Mario	**Silvia**
A.M.	**A.M.**
7:30 get up	**7:30** get up
8:00 watch TV	**8:00** listen to the radio
8:30 go to school	**8:30** go to school
P.M.	**P.M.**
12:00 have lunch	**12:00** have lunch
3:00 study at the library	**3:00** play basketball
4:00 go home	**4:00** visit her grandmother
5:00 do homework	**5:00** do homework
6:00 have dinner	**6:00** practice the guitar
7:00 play computer games	**7:00** make dinner
8:00 read the newspaper	**8:00** wash the dishes

1. At 7:30 A.M., _Mario and Silvia get up._

2. It's 8:00 A.M. _Mario is watching TV. Silvia is listening to the radio._

3. At 8:30 A.M., _____

4. It's noon. _____

5. At 3:00 P.M., _____

6. At 4:00 P.M., _____

7. It's 5:00 P.M. _____

8. At 6:00 P.M., _____

9. At 7:00 P.M., _____

10. It's 8:00 P.M. _____

6 AFFIRMATIVE AND NEGATIVE STATEMENTS

Read this letter from Mario. Mario made five mistakes in facts. Look at his schedule in Exercise 5. Then correct Mario's mistakes.

> Dear Carlo,
>
> ○ How are you? I'm really busy, so this is going to be a short letter. I get up at 7:00 every day. Then I listen to the radio for half an hour. (It helps my English comprehension.) After that, Silvia and I go to school. My classes are good. I'll tell you more about them in my next letter. Silvia and I have lunch together at noon. After classes, I study at the library. I go home at 4:00, but Silvia visits her grandfather.
>
> It's now 6:30. Silvia is practicing the piano. I usually have dinner at this time, but tonight I'm going to eat with Silvia. She doesn't make dinner until 7:00.
>
> ○ After dinner, I usually play computer games. Then I watch the news at 8:00. And that's my day!
>
> Let me know how you are.
>
> Mario

1. _He doesn't get up at 7:00._

He gets up at 7:30.

(continued on next page)

2. _____

_____

3. _____

_____

4. _____

_____

5. _____

_____

⑦ YES/NO QUESTIONS AND SHORT ANSWERS

Look at the schedules in Exercise 5. Ask and answer the questions.

1. (Mario and Silvia / go to school?)

   A: _Do Mario and Silvia go to school?_____

   B: _Yes, they do._____

2. (When / Mario and Silvia / get up?)

   A: _____

   B: _____

3. (Silvia / watch TV in the morning?)

   A: _____

   B: _____

4. It's 12:00. (What / they / do / now?)

   A: _____

   B: _____

5. It's 2:00. (Mario / study at the library now?)

   A: _____

   B: _____

6. (he / do his homework at school?)

   A: _____

   B: _____

7. (When / Silvia / play basketball?)

A: _____

B: _____

8. (Mario / play computer games before dinner?)

A: _____

B: _____

8 ADVERBS AND WORD ORDER

Put these words in the correct order to form statements. Use the correct form of the verb in parentheses.

1. Mario / the newspaper / (read) / always

    Mario always reads the newspaper.

2. on time / usually / Silvia / (be)

    _____

3. never / school / Silvia and Mario / (miss)

    _____

4. these days / they / (study) / English

    _____

5. usually / they / Italian / (speak)

    _____

6. (speak) / English / now / they

    _____

7. (do) / their homework / Silvia and Mario / always

    _____

8. (be) / Mario / tired / often

    _____

9. usually / (eat) / the students / in school / lunch

    _____

(continued on next page)

10. hungry / they / (be) / always

_____

11. Silvia / at the moment / (have) / a snack

_____

12. (go) / to bed / rarely / Silvia / late

_____

9 **EDITING**

Read this student's letter. Find and correct twelve mistakes in the use of the simple present tense and present progressive. The first mistake is already corrected.

Dear Andrew,

       'm writing
Hi, How are you? I ~~write~~ you this letter on the bus. I hope you can read my writing. They do some repairs on the road, so it's bumpy and the bus shakes. Guess what? I am having a job as a clerk in the mail room of a small company. The pay isn't good, but I'm liking the people there. They're all friendly, and we are speaking Spanish all the time. I'm also taking Spanish classes at night at a language institute. The class is meeting three times a week. It just started last week, so I'm not knowing many of the other students yet. They seem nice, though.

  I'm thinking that I'm beginning to get accustomed to living here. At first I experienced some "culture shock." I understand that this is quite normal. But these days I meet more and more people because of my job and my class, so I'm feeling more connected to things.

  What do you do these days? Do you still look for a new job?

  Please write when you can. I always like to hear from you.

           Yours,

           Brian

IMPERATIVE

---

① AFFIRMATIVE AND NEGATIVE IMPERATIVES

Complete the chart. Use the words in the box.

backward	in	~~left~~	loudly	off	slowly	tight
down	late	light	low	shut	small	up

Affirmative	**Negative**
1. Bend your *right* leg.	Don't bend your left leg.
2. _____	Don't look *up*.
3. Lean *forward*.	_____
4. _____	Don't take a *big* step.
5. Breathe *out*.	_____
6. _____	Don't count *quickly*.
7. Speak *softly*.	_____
8. _____	Don't keep your eyes *open*.
9. Wear *loose* clothes.	_____
10. _____	Don't wear *heavy* clothes.
11. Turn the lights *on*.	_____
12. _____	Don't turn the music *down*.
13. _____	Don't put the heat on *high*.
14. Come *early*.	_____

② AFFIRMATIVE AND NEGATIVE IMPERATIVES

Ada, a student, is asking her friends for directions to Jim's Gym. Look at the map and complete the conversation. Use the words in the box.

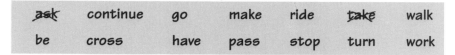

~~ask~~	continue	go	make	ride	~~take~~	walk
be	cross	have	pass	stop	turn	work

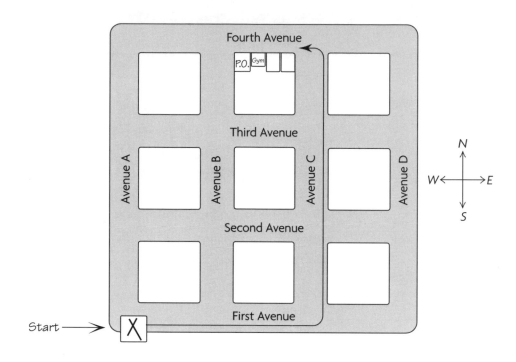

ADA: I'm going to take an exercise class at Jim's Gym. Do you know how to get there?

BOB: Jim's Gym? _____ Ask _____ Chen. He's taking a class there.
1.

ADA: I didn't know that. Which bus do you take to the gym, Chen?

CHEN: Oh, _____ don't take _____ the bus! It's not far from here.
2.

_____ or _____ your bike.
3.   4.

It's good exercise!

ADA: I'll walk. How do I get there?

CHEN: _____ two blocks east on First Avenue.
5.

ADA: East? You mean turn left?

CHEN: No. _____ left. Go right when you leave the building.
6.

OK? Then _____ a left turn when you get to Avenue C.
7.

_____ on Avenue C, but _____
8.   9.

when you reach Fourth Avenue. _____ Fourth Avenue.
10.

It's another left at Fourth. But _____ careful. Jim's Gym
11.

is small and it's easy to miss. _____ the post office. The
12.

gym is right before it.

ADA: Thanks.

CHEN: Sure. _____ fun! _____ too hard!
13.   14.

---

❸ EDITING

Read Ada's note to her roommate. Find and correct five mistakes in the use of imperatives. The first mistake is already corrected.

Sara,

Call
Your mother called. ~~Calls~~ her at your sister's tonight.

Don't you call after 10:00, though.

I went to the gym.

Wash please the dishes and threw out the trash.

If anyone calls for me, takes a message.

Thanks a lot.
A.

---

❹ PERSONALIZATION

Draw a map and give directions to a place near you. Use your own paper.

SIMPLE PAST TENSE

1 SPELLING: REGULAR AND IRREGULAR VERBS

Write the simple past tense form of the verbs.

Base Form	Simple Past	Base Form	Simple Past
1. answer	answered	13. live	_____
2. buy	bought	14. meet	_____
3. catch	_____	15. need	_____
4. do	_____	16. open	_____
5. look	_____	17. put	_____
6. find	_____	18. read	_____
7. give	_____	19. say	_____
8. hurry	_____	20. think	_____
9. see	_____	21. understand	_____
10. die	_____	22. vote	_____
11. kiss	_____	23. win	_____
12. come	_____	24. feel	_____

25. The past of *be* is _____ or _____.

2 AFFIRMATIVE AND NEGATIVE STATEMENTS: *BE*

Look at the chart of famous writers of the past. Complete the sentences with **was**, **wasn't**, **were**, *and* **weren't**.

Isaak Babel	1894-1941	Russia	short-story writer, playwright*
James Baldwin	1924-1987	United States	author, playwright
Honoré de Balzac	1799-1850	France	novelist
Simone de Beauvoir	1908-1966	France	novelist, essayist**
Giovanni Boccaccio	1313-1375	Italy	poet, storyteller
Karel Čapek	1890-1938	Czechoslovakia	novelist, essayist
Agatha Christie	1890-1976	England	mystery writer
Lorraine Hansberry	1930-1965	United States	playwright
Pablo Neruda	1904-1973	Chile	poet

*A *playwright* is a person who writes plays. **An *essayist* is a person who writes essays.

1. Simone de Beauvoir _____wasn't_____ a French poet. She _____was_____ a French novelist.

2. Giovanni Boccaccio _____ born in 1313.

3. James Baldwin and Lorraine Hansberry _____ American poets. They _____ playwrights.

4. Karel Čapek _____ a poet.

5. Pablo Neruda _____ from Chile.

6. Honoré de Balzac _____ a playwright. He _____ a novelist.

7. Agatha Christie _____ American. She _____ English.

8. Isaak Babel _____ Russian. He _____ French.

9. Simone de Beauvoir and Honoré de Balzac _____ both French.

10. Pablo Neruda and Simone de Beauvoir _____ both born in the early 1900s.

3 QUESTIONS AND ANSWERS WITH THE PAST TENSE OF *BE*

Ask and answer questions about the people in Exercise 2. Use **was** *and* **wasn't**.

1. James Baldwin / a playwright?

   A: _Was James Baldwin a playwright?_____

   B: _Yes, he was._____

2. Where / Simone de Beauvoir from?

   A: _____

   B: _____

3. What nationality / Pablo Neruda?

   A: _____

   B: _____

4. Who / Boccaccio?

   A: _____

   B: _____

5. Agatha Christie / French?

   A: _____

   B: _____

6. What nationality / Lorraine Hansberry?

   A: _____

   B: _____

(continued on next page)

7. Honoré de Balzac / a poet?

A: _____

B: _____

8. When / Karel Čapek / born?

A: _____

B: _____

9. Who / Isaak Babel?

A: _____

B: _____

4 AFFIRMATIVE STATEMENTS

Complete these short biographies. Use the simple past tense form of the verbs in the boxes.

| ~~be~~ | die | include | spend | translate | write |

1. Lin Yutang (1895–1976) _____was_____ a Chinese-American writer.
                                      1.
He _____ most of his life in the United States. Dr. Lin
        2.
_____ a lot about his native China. His books
    3.
_____ several novels. He also _____ other
    4.   **5.**
people's works. Lin _____ at the age of 81.
                          6.

| be | begin | call | have | live | paint |

2. Anna Mary Robertson Moses (1860–1961) _____ an
                                                    1.
American painter. She _____ on a farm in New York State.
                            2.
Because she _____ painting in her seventies, people
                  3.
_____ her Grandma Moses. She never _____ any
    4.   **5.**
formal art training. Moses _____ simple, colorful scenes of
                                6.
farm life.

be	build	fly	last	take place	watch

3. Orville Wright (1871–1948) and **Wilbur Wright** (1867–1912)

_____ American airplane inventors. The two brothers
　　　1.

_____ their first planes in their bicycle shop in Ohio. On
　　　2.

December 17, 1903, Orville _____ their plane, *Flyer 1*, a
　　　　　　　　　　　　　　　　3.

distance of 120 feet. Wilbur, four men, and a boy _____
　　　　　　　　　　　　　　　　　　　　　　　　4.

from the ground. This first controlled, power-driven flight

_____ near Kitty Hawk, North Carolina. It _____
　　　5.　　　　　　　　　　　　　　　　　　　　　　　　6.

only about 12 seconds.

❺ QUESTIONS AND ANSWERS

Ask and answer questions about the people in Exercise 4.

Biography 1

1. When / Lin Yutang / live?

   A: ___When did Lin Yutang live?_____

   B: ___He lived from 1895 to 1976._____

2. What / he / do?

   A: _____

   B: _____

3. he / write poetry?

   A: _____

   B: _____

4. Where / he / spend most of his life?

   A: _____

   B: _____

(continued on next page)

Biography 2

5. What / people / call Anna Mary Robertson Moses?

    A: _____

    B: _____

6. What / she / do?

    A: _____

    B: _____

7. When / she / begin painting?

    A: _____

    B: _____

8. she / have formal art training?

    A: _____

    B: _____

Biography 3

9. Where / the Wright brothers / build their first planes?

    A: _____

    B: _____

10. both brothers / fly the *Flyer 1*?

    A: _____

    B: _____

11. Where / first controlled flight / take place?

    A: _____

    B: _____

12. How long / the flight / last?

    A: _____

    B: _____

6 NEGATIVE STATEMENTS

There were a lot of similarities between the Wright brothers. But there were also differences. Complete the chart about the differences between Orville and Wilbur.

Orville	**Wilbur**
1. Orville talked a lot.	Wilbur didn't talk a lot.
2. Orville didn't spend a lot of time alone.	Wilbur spent a lot of time alone.
3. _____	Wilbur had serious health problems.
4. Orville grew a moustache.	_____
5. _____	Wilbur lost most of his hair.
6. Orville took courses in Latin.	_____
7. Orville liked to play jokes.	_____
8. Orville dressed very fashionably.	_____
9. Orville played the guitar.	_____
10. _____	Wilbur built the first glider.
11. _____	Wilbur made the first attempts to fly.
12. _____	Wilbur chose the location of Kitty Hawk.
13. Orville had a lot of patience.	_____
14. Orville lived a long life.	_____

7 EDITING

Read this student's short biography of a famous person. Find and correct six mistakes in the use of the simple past tense. The first mistake is already corrected.

> ***Pablo Neruda*** *(1904–1973) Pablo Neruda* ~~were~~ was *a famous poet, political activist, and diplomat. He was born in Parral, Chile. When he was seventeen, he gone to Santiago to continue his education. He did not finished, but he soon published his first book. Neruda spends the next several decades traveling and continuing to write poetry. In 1971, while he was Chile's ambassador to France, he winned the Nobel Prize in literature. He dead two years later.*

USED TO

1 AFFIRMATIVE STATEMENTS

Life in the United States isn't the way it used to be. Complete the chart.

	In the Past	Now
1.	People used to ride horses.	People ride in cars.
2.	_____ by candlelight.	People read by electric light.
3.	_____ over open fires.	People cook in microwave ovens.
4.	_____ in propeller airplanes.	People fly in jet planes.
5.	_____ large families.	People have small families.
6.	_____ all of their clothes by hand.	People wash most of their clothes in washing machines.
7.	_____ manual typewriters.	People use word processors and computers.
8.	_____ twenty-five days to get a message from New York to San Francisco.	It takes just a few seconds.

2 AFFIRMATIVE AND NEGATIVE STATEMENTS

*Complete the sentences about the assistant manager of a California bank, Yoko Shimizu. Use **used to** or **didn't use to** and the verbs in parentheses ( ).*

1. Yoko _____used to be_____ a full-time student. Now she
   (be)
   has a job at a bank.

2. She _____ with a computer. Now she uses one
   (work)
   every day.

3. She _____ a car. Now she owns a 1999 Toyota Corolla.
   (have)

4. Yoko _____ the bus to work. Now she drives.
   (take)

5. The bus _____ crowded. These days it's hard to find a seat.
   (be)

6. Yoko _____ in New York. Then she moved to Los Angeles.
   (live)

7. She _____ Los Angeles. Now she thinks it's a nice city.
   (like)

8. She _____ a lot of people in Los Angeles. Now she has a lot
   (know)
   of friends there.

9. She _____ to New York several times a year. These days she
   (return)
   doesn't go there very often.

10. She _____ a lot of letters. Now she makes a lot of phone
    (write)
    calls instead.

---

3 **QUESTIONS AND ANSWERS**

*Look at these two ID cards. Ask and answer questions about Sara
Rogers, a new employee at City Savings Bank. Use* **used to** *and the cues
in parentheses ( ).*

THEN

CITY COLLEGE

[ ] Ms.
[ ] Mr.
[x] Mrs.
[ ] Miss   Sara Rogers-Gordon
            Name
Address: 20 E. 15 St.
         New York, NY 10003
STUDENT ID

NOW

CITY SAVINGS BANK *Employee ID*

[x] Ms.
[ ] Mr.
[ ] Mrs.
[ ] Miss   *Sara Rogers*
            Name
Address: *5432 Orange St.*
         Los Angeles, CA 90048   *$*

(continued on next page)

1. (live in California?)

   A: _Did she use to live in California?_

   B: _No, she didn't._

2. Sara recently moved to Los Angeles. (Where / live?)

   A: _____

   B: _____

3. This is her first job. (What / do?)

   A: _____

   B: _____

4. Sara looks very different from before. She has short hair and wears glasses. (have long hair?)

   A: _____

   B: _____

5. (wear glasses?)

   A: _____

   B: _____

6. Sara's last name is different from before. (be married?)

   A: _____

   B: _____

7. (use *Ms.* before her name?)

   A: _____

   B: _____

4 EDITING

*Read this student's journal entry. Find and correct five mistakes in the use of **used to**. The first mistake is already corrected.*

Journal

Sunday, Oct. 5

    Today I ran into an old classmate. At first, I almost didn't recognize him! He looked so
                  have
different. He used to ~~had~~ very dark hair. Now he's almost all gray. He also used to being a little

heavy. Now he's quite thin. And he was wearing a suit and tie! I couldn't believe it. He never

use to dress that way. He only used to wear jeans! His personality seemed different, too. He

didn't used to talk very much. Now he seems very outgoing.

    I wonder what he thought about me! I'm sure I look and act a lot different from the way I

was used to, too!

5 PERSONALIZATION

*Write five sentences about how your life used to be different from the way it is now. Use **used to**.*

1. _____

2. _____

3. _____

4. _____

5. _____

PAST PROGRESSIVE AND SIMPLE PAST TENSE

① AFFIRMATIVE AND NEGATIVE STATEMENTS WITH THE PAST PROGRESSIVE

Frank Cotter is a financial manager. Look at his schedule and complete the sentences.

10 Wednesday

9:00–10:00	meet with Ms. Jacobs
10:00–11:00	write financial reports
11:00–12:00	answer correspondence
12:00–1:00	eat lunch with Mr. Webb at Sol's Cafe
1:00–3:00	attend lecture at City University
3:00–4:00	discuss budget with Alan
4:00–5:00	return phone calls

1. At 9:30 Mr. Cotter _____ was meeting with _____ Ms. Jacobs.

2. At 9:30 he _____ financial reports.

3. At 11:30 he _____ correspondence.

4. At 12:30 he and Mr. Webb _____ lunch.

5. They _____ at Frank's Diner.

6. At 2:00 he _____ a lecture.

7. At 3:30 he and Alan _____ reports.

8. They _____ the budget.

9. At 4:30 he _____ correspondence.

10. He _____ phone calls.

② QUESTIONS AND ANSWERS WITH THE PAST PROGRESSIVE

Look at the schedule in Exercise 1. Ask questions and give short answers.

1. Mr. Cotter / meet / with Mr. Webb at 9:30?

   A: ___Was Mr. Cotter meeting with Mr. Webb at 9:30?___

   B: ___No, he wasn't.___

2. What / he / do at 9:30?

   A: _____

   B: _____

3. Mr. Cotter / write police reports at 10:30?

   A: _____

   B: _____

4. What kind of reports / he / write?

   A: _____

   B: _____

5. What / he / do at 11:30?

   A: _____

   B: _____

6. he / have lunch at 12:00?

   A: _____

   B: _____

7. Who / eat lunch with him?

   A: _____

   B: _____

(continued on next page)

8. Where / they / have lunch?

A: _____

B: _____

9. Who / he / talk to at 3:30?

A: _____

B: _____

10. What / they / discuss?

A: _____

B: _____

③ STATEMENTS WITH THE PAST PROGRESSIVE AND SIMPLE PAST TENSE

*Read about an explosion at the World Trade Center in New York City.
Complete the story with the past progressive or simple past tense form
of the verbs in parentheses ( ).*

On February 26, 1993, a bomb _____exploded_____ in New York City's World
                            1. (explode)

Trade Center. At the time, 55,000 people _____were working_____ in the Twin Towers,
                                         2. (work)

and thousands of others _____ the 110-story world-famous tourist
                        3. (visit)

attraction.

The explosion, which _____ a little after noon, _____ six
                     4. (take place)   **5. (kill)**

people and _____ more than a thousand others. It _____ all
           6. (injure)   **7. (take)**

day and half the night to get everyone out of the building.

When the bomb _____, the lights _____, the elevators
              8. (explode)   **9. (go out)**

_____, and fires _____. Many people were in the wrong place
   10. (stop)   **11. (start)**

at the wrong time. Four co-workers _____ lunch in their offices when
                12. (eat)

the explosion _____ the Twin Towers. When the blast _____,
      13. (shake)   **14. (occur)**

the building's walls _____ and the ceilings _____. Rescue
      15. (crumble)   **16. (collapse)**

workers _____ within fifteen minutes and _____ the four
      17. (arrive)   **18. (find)**

workers dead.

   One man _____ in the garage beneath the World Trade Center when
         19. (walk)

the bomb _____. He _____ a heart attack while rescue
     20. (go off)   **21. (have)**

workers _____ him to the ambulance.
     22. (carry)

   Sixty schoolchildren were luckier. They _____ the huge elevators
                 23. (ride)

when the lights _____ and the elevators _____. The children
     24. (go out)   **25. (stop)**

and their teachers _____ stand in the hot, dark space as they waited
     26. (have to)

for help. Six hours later, when the elevator _____ the ground floor, the
           27. (reach)

school bus driver _____ for them. He _____ the children
     28. (wait)   **29. (drive)**

home to their worried families. How did the children feel while all this

_____? "We were scared," they answered.
   30. (happen)

   This is one class trip they will never forget.

4 QUESTIONS WITH THE PAST PROGRESSIVE AND SIMPLE PAST TENSE

Reporters are interviewing people about the explosion at the World Trade Center. Use the past progressive and the simple past tense to write the interview questions.

1. What / you do / when you feel the explosion?

   A: <u>What were you doing when you felt the explosion?</u>

   B: I was sitting in my chair.

2. What happen / when the bomb explode?

   A: _____

   B: I flew off my chair and landed on the floor.

3. What / the schoolchildren do / when the lights go out?

   A: _____

   B: They were riding the elevator.

4. How many people / work in the building / when the bomb explode?

   A: _____

   B: Approximately 55,000.

5. Six World Trade Center workers were killed. What / they do / when the bomb go off?

   A: _____

   B: They were having lunch in their offices.

6. What happen to the offices / when the blast occur?

   A: _____

   B: The walls crumbled and the ceilings collapsed.

7. There was a man in the garage. What / he do / when the bomb explode?

   A: _____

   B: He was walking to his car.

8. What happen / when the rescue workers / bring him to the ambulance?

   A: _____

   B: He had a heart attack before they got him in the ambulance.

FUTURE

1 AFFIRMATIVE STATEMENTS WITH *BE GOING TO*

*Read the following situations. Write a prediction. Use **be going to** and the correct information from the box.*

crash	get a ticket	make a left turn	~~take a trip~~
eat lunch	get gas	rain	wash the car

1. Mr. Medina is carrying two suitcases toward his car.

   <u>He's going to take a trip.</u>

2. Ms. Marshall has a bucket of water, soap, and a sponge.

   _____

3. Mr. and Mrs. Johnson are driving into an Exxon service station.

   _____

4. Fred is driving behind a woman in a black sports car. Her left indicator light is flashing.

   _____

5. Tiffany is driving 70 miles per hour in a 50-mile-per-hour zone. A police officer is right behind her.

   _____

6. A blue Ford is driving directly toward a white Toyota. They don't have time to stop.

   _____

7. It's noon. The Smiths are driving into a Burger King parking lot.

   _____

8. The sky is full of dark clouds.

   _____

② QUESTIONS WITH *BE GOING TO*

Write questions using the cues.

1. What / you / do this summer?

   A: ___What are you going to do this summer?_____

   B: My wife and I are going to take a trip to San Francisco.

2. How long / you / stay?

   A: _____

   B: Just for a week.

3. you / stay at a hotel?

   A: _____

   B: Yes. We're staying at a hotel in North Beach.

4. What / you / do in San Francisco?

   A: _____

   B: Oh, the usual, I suppose. Sightseeing and shopping.

5. you / visit Fisherman's Wharf?

   A: _____

   B: Yes. We're going to take one of those city bus tours.

6. your daughter / go with you?

   A: _____

   B: No, she's going to attend summer school. Our son isn't going either.

7. What / he / do?

   A: _____

   B: He got a job at Burger King.

8. When / you / leave?

   A: _____

   B: June 11.

   A: Have a good trip.

   B: Thanks.

3 AFFIRMATIVE AND NEGATIVE STATEMENTS WITH *BE GOING TO*

Look at Mr. and Mrs. Medina's boarding passes. Then read the following sentences. All of them have incorrect information. Correct the information.

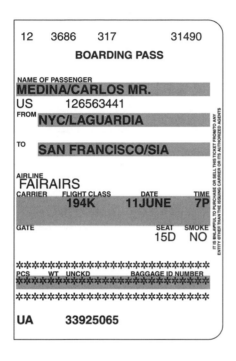
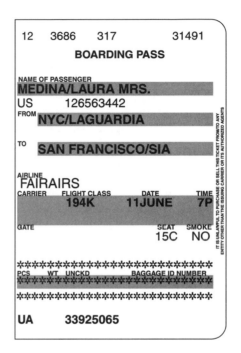

1. Mr. Medina is going to go to Los Angeles.

    He isn't going to go to Los Angeles.

    He's going to go to San Francisco.

2. He's going to take the train.

3. He's going to travel alone.

4. The Medinas are going to leave from Chicago.

(continued on next page)

5. They're going to fly US Airways.

_____

_____

6. They're going to leave on July 11.

_____

_____

7. The plane is going to depart at 7:00 A.M.

_____

_____

8. The Medinas are going to sit apart.

_____

_____

9. They are going to be in a smoking section.

_____

_____

10. Mrs. Medina is going to sit in seat 15B.

_____

_____

④ AFFIRMATIVE AND NEGATIVE STATEMENTS, QUESTIONS, AND SHORT ANSWERS WITH *WILL*

Mrs. Medina is reading the airplane magazine. Complete this magazine interview about personal robots. Use **will** *or* **won't** *and the verbs in parentheses ( ).*

INTERVIEWER: We all know that robots are already working in factories. But tell

us something about the future. _____Will_____ people

_____have_____ robots at home?
   1. (have)
SCIENTIST: Yes, they _____. I believe that personal robots
   2.

_____ as common in the home as personal computers

3. (become)

are today.

INTERVIEWER: _____ they _____ the computer?

4. (replace)

SCIENTIST: No, they _____ the computer, but one day robots

5. (replace)

_____ probably _____ computers.

6. (operate)

INTERVIEWER: Amazing! What other things _____ personal robots

_____?

7. (do)

SCIENTIST: Well, for one thing, they _____ complete home

8. (be)

entertainment centers. They _____, they

9. (sing)

_____ . . .

10. (dance)

INTERVIEWER: _____ they _____ jokes?

11. (tell)

SCIENTIST: Yes, they _____! But, as with humans, they

12.

_____ always _____ funny!

13. (be)

INTERVIEWER: What else _____ the personal robot _____?

14. (do)

_____ it _____ more serious uses?

15. (have)

SCIENTIST: Yes, it _____. Robots _____ probably

16.

_____ care for this country's aging population. They

17. (help)

_____ people, but they _____ some of the more

18. (replace)   **19. (perform)**

routine activities such as vacuuming and loading the dishwasher.

INTERVIEWER: It all sounds great. Do you predict any problems?

SCIENTIST: Unfortunately, yes. Some people _____ happy with the

20. (be)

spread of robots. Not everyone's life _____. Some people

21. (improve)

_____ their jobs to robots. And other people

22. (lose)

_____ criminal robots!

23. (create)

INTERVIEWER: _____ we _____ new laws to deal with robotic

24. (need)

crime?

SCIENTIST: I'm afraid so.

(continued on next page)

INTERVIEWER: Tell me, how _____ these personal robots

_____?
25. (look)

SCIENTIST: Well, they _____ exactly like humans, but they
26. (look)

_____ them.
27. (resemble)

INTERVIEWER: And when _____ all this _____?
28. (happen)

SCIENTIST: Soon! I predict it _____ in the very near future.
29. (happen)

---

5 RECOGNIZING THE SIMPLE PRESENT AND PRESENT PROGRESSIVE WHEN THEY REFER TO THE FUTURE

Read this article about a new play. Underline the simple present tense verbs and present progressive verbs only when they refer to the future.

A NEW PLAY

BATS

Next Wednesday <u>is</u> the first performance of *Bats*. Melissa Robins is playing the leading role. Robins, who lives in Italy and who is vacationing in Greece, is not available for an interview at this time. She is, however, appearing on Channel 8's "Theater Talk" sometime next month.

Although shows traditionally begin at 8:00 P.M., *Bats*, because of its length, starts a half-hour earlier.

Immediately following the opening-night performance, the company is having a reception in the theater lounge. Tickets are still available. Call 555-6310 for more information.

---

6 CONTRAST OF FUTURE FORMS

Read the conversations and circle the most appropriate future forms.

1. **A:** Do you know our arrival time?

   B: According to the schedule, (we arrive)/ we'll arrive at 10:45.

2. **A:** Why did you bring your computer with you?

   B: <u>I'll do / I'm going to do</u> some work while we're away.

3. A: I'm thirsty. I think <u>I'll ask / I'm asking</u> for a Coke.

   B: Good idea. There's the flight attendant.

4. A: Excuse me. Do you know what the weather's like in San Francisco?

   B: It's clear now, but <u>it's raining / it's going to rain</u> tomorrow.

5. A: Which movie <u>will they show / are they showing</u>?

   B: The latest *Star Wars*. Have you seen it?

6. A: Just look at those dark clouds!

   B: I see. It looks like <u>we're going to have / we'll have</u> some rough weather ahead.

7. A: I'm tired. I think <u>I'll take / I'm taking</u> a little nap. Wake me when the movie begins.

   B: OK. Sweet dreams.

8. A: It's 11:00 P.M. already!

   B: I know. <u>We're going to arrive / We arrive</u> late.

9. A: You know, I don't think the airport buses run after midnight.

   B: I'm afraid you're right. How <u>are we going to get / are we getting</u> to the hotel?

10. A: Hmm. No buses. Well, that's no problem. <u>We'll take / We're going to take</u> a taxi instead.

   B: Good idea.

11. A: I missed the announcement. What did the captain say?

   B: He said, "Fasten your seat belts. <u>We're landing / We'll land</u> in about ten minutes."

12. C: How long <u>are you going to stay / will you stay</u> in San Francisco?

   A & B: Just a week.

   C: Well, enjoy yourselves. And thank you for flying FairAirs.

7 EDITING

Read this boy's postcard. Find and correct five mistakes in the use of future forms. The first mistake is already corrected. Note: There may be more than one way to correct the mistakes!

> # Greetings from
> # San Francisco!
>
> Hi!
>
>   'm
> I going to stay here for a week with my parents.
>
> We have a lot of fun things planned. Tomorrow night we'll see
>
> a play called <u>Bats</u>. Mom already bought tickets for it. The play
>
> begins at 8:00, and before that we have dinner on Fisherman's
>
> Wharf. Right now we're sitting in Golden Gate Park, but we
>
> have to leave. It has suddenly gotten very cloudy. It will rain!
>
>   I call you soon.
>
>   Jason

FUTURE TIME CLAUSES

1 SIMPLE PRESENT TENSE OR FUTURE WITH *WILL*

Complete the clauses with the correct form of the verbs in parentheses ( ).
Then match each time clause to a main clause.

Time Clause	**Main Clause**
_h_ **1.** When the alarm clock _____rings_____, (ring)	**a.** they _____ very (be) tired.
___ **2.** As soon as the coffee _____ ready, (be)	**b.** she _____. (drive)
___ **3.** When they _____ (finish) breakfast,	**c.** they _____ it. (drink)
___ **4.** After her husband _____ the dishes, (wash)	**d.** they _____ their (fasten) seat belts.
___ **5.** As soon as they _____ (get in) the car,	**e.** she _____ them. (dry)
___ **6.** Until he _____ his (get) driver's license,	**f.** they _____ their (need) umbrellas.
___ **7.** Until the rain _____, (stop)	**g.** they _____ the (do) dishes.
___ **8.** By the time the day _____ over, (be)	**h.** she ____ _'ll get up._ ____ (get up)

❷ SIMPLE PRESENT OR FUTURE (*WILL / BE GOING TO*) AND TIME EXPRESSIONS

Vera is a student. Look at her future plans. Complete the sentences below with the correct form of the verbs in parentheses ( ) and choose the correct time expression.

Future Plans

○   *Take the TOEFL®* exam*

       Apply to college for next year

       Finish school

       Visit Aunt Isabel at Shadybrook

       Get a summer job and take a computer-programming course

       Fly to Brazil — Aug. 28

       Get married! — Sept. 30

○   *Return to the United States*

       *TOEFL® = Test of English as a Foreign Language

---

1. Vera _____will take_____ the TOEFL exam _____before_____ she _____applies_____ to college.
       (take)   **(when / before)**   **(apply)**

2. Vera _____ to college _____ she _____ school.
       (apply)   **(before / after)**   **(finish)**

3. _____ she _____ school, she _____ her aunt.
   (Before / After)   **(finish)**   **(visit)**

4. _____ she _____ at a summer job, she _____ a course
   (Before / While)   **(work)**   **(take)**
in computer programming.

5. She _____ her aunt _____ she _____ a summer job.
       (visit)   **(while / before)**   **(get)**

6. _____ she _____ the course, she _____ to Brazil.
   (Before / When)   **(finish)**   **(fly)**

7. She _____ _____ she _____ in Brazil.
    (get married)   **(when / before)**   **(be)**

8. She _____ to the United States _____ she _____.
     (return)   **(before / after)**   **(get married)**

3 SIMPLE PRESENT TENSE OR FUTURE

Vera's aunt lives at Shadybrook Retirement Village. Complete this ad for Shadybrook. Use the correct form of the verbs in parentheses ( ).

Shadybrook
Retirement Village

What _____will_____ you _____do_____ when you
1. (do)
_____? Where _____ you _____ when
2. (retire)   3. (go)
you finally_____ all that free time?
4. (have)
By the time you _____ 65, you probably _____
5. (turn)   6. (want)
to make some major life changes. Here at *Shadybrook Retirement*

Village, you can enjoy swimming, tennis, golf, and much more.

Come and see for yourself. After you _____ us, you
7. (visit)
_____ to leave!
8. (not want)

4 SENTENCE COMBINING

Combine these sentences. Use the simple present tense and future forms
*(**will / be going to**).*

1. Vera will finish her summer job. Then she's going to fly to Brazil.

   ___Vera is going to fly to Brazil___ after ___she finishes her summer job.___

2. Vera will save enough money from her summer job. Then she's going to buy a plane

   ticket.

   As soon as _____

(continued on next page)

3. Vera's going to buy presents for her family. Then she's going to go home.

Before _____

4. Vera will arrive at the airport. Her father will be there to drive her home.

When _____

5. Vera and her father will get home. They'll immediately have dinner.

As soon as _____

6. They'll finish dinner. Then Vera will give her family the presents.

_____ after _____

7. Vera's brother will wash the dishes, and Vera's sister will dry them.

_____ while _____

8. The whole family will stay up talking. Then the clock will strike midnight.

_____ until _____

9. They'll all feel very tired. Then they'll go to bed.

By the time _____

10. Vera's head will hit the pillow, and she'll fall asleep immediately.

_____ as soon as _____

5 PERSONALIZATION

Complete these sentences with information about your own future plans.

1. As soon as _____, I'll go to bed.

2. Before I take a break, _____.

3. Until _____, I'll stay in school.

4. When I save enough money, _____.

5. I won't _____ before I _____.

6. _____ after _____.

7. _____ while _____.

8. When I finish this exercise, _____.

WH- QUESTIONS:
SUBJECT AND PREDICATE

1 SUBJECT QUESTIONS

Ask questions about the words in italics. Use **What, Whose, Who,** *or* **How many.**

1. *Something* happened last night.

   <u>What happened last night?</u>

2. *Someone's* phone rang at midnight.

   _____

3. *Someone* was calling for Michelle.

   _____

4. *Someone* was having a party.

   _____

5. *Some number of* people left the party.

   _____

6. *Something* surprised them.

   _____

7. *Someone's* friend called the police.

   _____

8. *Some number of* police arrived.

   _____

9. *Something* happened next.

   _____

10. *Someone* told the police about a theft.

    _____

39

(continued on next page)

11. *Someone's* jewelry disappeared.

_____

12. *Some number of* necklaces vanished.

_____

❷ PREDICATE QUESTIONS

Use the cues to write questions about Megan Knight, an accountant in Texas. Then match each question to its correct answer.

Questions	Answers
1. Where / she / live?	**a.** Two years.
_____Where does she live?_____ _e_	
2. How many rooms / her apartment / have?	**b.** By bus.
_____ ____	
3. How much rent / she / pay?	**c.** The first of the month.
_____ ____	
4. When / she / pay the rent?	**d.** Ling, Jackson, & Drew, Inc.
_____ ____	
5. Who / she / live with?	**e.** In Texas.
_____ ____	
6. What / she / do?	**f.** Five and a half.
_____ ____	
7. Which company / she / work for?	**g.** She's an accountant.
_____ ____	
8. How long / she / plan to stay there?	**h.** Her sister.
_____ ____	
9. How / she / get to work?	**i.** Because she doesn't like to drive.
_____ ____	
10. Why / she / take the bus?	**j.** About $800 a month.
_____ ____	

❸ SUBJECT AND PREDICATE QUESTIONS

Megan wrote a letter to her friend, Janice. The letter got wet, and now
Janice can't read some parts of it. What questions does Janice ask to get
the missing information?

Dear Janice,

Hi! I just moved to ▮▮▮▮ .[1] I
left Chicago because ▮▮▮▮▮▮ .[2]
▮▮▮▮▮▮▮▮▮ .[3] moved with me,
and we are sharing an apartment.
I got a job in a ▮▮▮▮▮▮▮ .[4]
It started ▮▮▮▮▮ .[5] The people
seem nice.

Our apartment is great. It has
▮▮▮▮ [6] rooms. ▮▮▮▮ of the
rooms came with carpeting, but two
of them have beautiful wood floors.
The rent isn't too high, either. We
each pay $ ▮▮▮ a month.

We need to buy som▮ ▮▮▮▮ .[9]
▮▮▮▮▮ 's[10] brother wants to visit
her, so we really need an extra bed.

By the way, ▮▮▮▮▮ [11] called
last Sunday. I also spoke to
▮▮▮▮▮ .[12] They want to visit us
in ▮▮▮▮ .[13]

Would you like to come, too?
Is that a good time for you?
There's plenty of room because
▮▮▮▮▮▮▮▮ .[14] Write and
let me know.

Love,
Megan

---

1. _Where did you move?_

2. _____

3. _____

4. _____

5. _____

6. _____

7. _____

8. _____

9. _____

10. _____

11. _____

12. _____

13. _____

14. _____

UNIT

REFLEXIVE AND RECIPROCAL PRONOUNS

1 REFLEXIVE PRONOUNS

Write the reflexive pronouns.

1. I   _____myself_____

2. my grandfather   _____

3. the children   _____

4. the class   _____

5. my aunt   _____

6. you   _____ OR _____

7. people   _____

8. life   _____

9. my parents   _____

10. we   _____

2 REFLEXIVE AND RECIPROCAL PRONOUNS

Circle the correct pronouns to complete these sentences.

1. Cindi and Jim phone (each other) / themselves every weekend.

2. They have worked with each other / themselves for five years.

3. Cindi herself / himself has been with the same company for ten years.

4. It's a nice place to work. All of the employees consider one another / themselves lucky to be working there.

5. They respect each other / each other's opinions.

6. The boss herself / itself is very nice.

7. She tells her employees, "Don't push <u>themselves / yourselves</u> too hard!"

8. Cindi enjoys the job <u>herself / itself</u>, but she especially likes her co-workers.

9. My brother and I are considering applying for a job there <u>myself / ourselves</u>.

10. We talk to <u>each other / ourselves</u> about it when we jog together.

---

3 REFLEXIVE AND RECIPROCAL PRONOUNS

*Read the conversations. Complete the summary with appropriate
reflexive and reciprocal pronouns and forms of the verbs in parentheses.*

1. **JOYCE:** This party is a lot of fun.
    HANK: I've never danced with so many people in my life!

    SUMMARY: Joyce and Hank _____ are enjoying themselves _____.
    (enjoy)

2. **CARA:** You know, you're really easy to talk to.
    MAX: I feel the same way. I feel like we've known each other a long time.

    SUMMARY: Cara and Max _____ company.
    (enjoy)

3. **GINA:** I'm so glad you could come. There are food and drinks on that table over
       there. Why don't you take a plate and get some?
    CHEN: Thanks. I will. It all looks delicious.

    SUMMARY: Chen _____.
    (help)

4. **AMY:** OK, Amy. Now don't be shy. Go over and talk to him.
    TIM: Come on, Tim. You can do it. She's looking in your direction. Just go on over.

    SUMMARY: Amy and Tim _____.
    (talk)

5. **AMY:** Hi. I'm Amy.
    TIM: Hi. I'm Tim.

    SUMMARY: Amy and Tim _____.
    (introduce)

6. **AMY:** So, how do you know Gina?
    TIM: Oh, Gina and I were in the same class. What about you?

    SUMMARY: Amy and Tim _____.
    (talk)

7. **PAT:** Did you come with Doug?
    LAURA: No. Doug couldn't make it, but he let me use his car.

    SUMMARY: Laura _____.
    (drive)

8. **LIZ:** I'm sorry to hear about your job, Hank.
    HANK: I think I didn't take it seriously enough, but I've learned my lesson. I'll do
       better next time.

    SUMMARY: Hank _____.
    (blame)

(continued on next page)

9.   **Ron:** We were late because you forgot the address.
      Mia: It's not my fault. You never gave me the slip of paper!

  Summary: Ron and Mia _____.
                                                (criticize)

10.   **Liz:** It was a wonderful party. Thanks for inviting me.
      Gina: Thanks for coming. And thank you for the lovely flowers.

  Summary: Liz and Gina _____.
                                              (thank)

 **EDITING**

Read Liz's journal entry. Find and correct nine mistakes in the use of reflexive and reciprocal pronouns. The first mistake is already corrected.

April 25

                              myself
I really enjoyed ~~me~~ at Gina's party! Hank was there and we talked to ourselves quite a bit. He's a little depressed about losing his job. He thinks it's all his own fault, and he blames him for the whole thing. Hank introduced myself to several of his friends. I spoke a lot to this one woman, Cara. We have a lot of things in common, and after just an hour, we felt like we had known each other's forever. Cara, himself, is a computer programmer, just like me.

    At first I was nervous about going to the party alone. I sometimes feel a little uncomfortable when I'm in a social situation by oneself. But this time was different. Before I went, I kept telling myself to relax. My roommate, too, kept telling myself, "Don't be so hard on you! Just have fun!" That's what I advised Hank to do, too. Before we left the party, Hank and I promised us to keep in touch. I hope to see him again soon.

PHRASAL VERBS

1 PARTICLES

Complete the chart.

Phrasal Verb	Definition
1. take ___off___	*remove*
2. figure _____	*solve*
3. go _____	*continue*
4. call _____	*cancel*
5. call _____	*phone*
6. fill _____	*complete*
7. turn _____	*reject*
8. point _____	*indicate*
9. grow _____	*become an adult*
10. give _____	*quit*
11. help _____	*assist*
12. blow _____	*explode*
13. look _____	*be careful*
14. come _____	*enter*
15. work _____	*exercise*

② PHRASAL VERBS

Complete the handout. Use the correct phrasal verbs from the box.

do over	hand in	help out	look over	look up
pick out	~~pick up~~	set up	talk over	write up

Science 101   Instructions for Writing the Term Paper   Prof. Cho

....

1. _____Pick up_____ a list of topics from the science department secretary.

2. _____ a topic that interests you. (If you are having problems choosing a

   topic, I'll be glad to _____ you _____.)

3. Go to the library. _____ information on your chosen topic.

4. _____ an appointment with me to _____ your topic.

5. _____ your first draft.

6. _____ it _____ carefully. Check for accuracy of facts,

   spelling, and grammar errors.

7. _____ your report _____ if necessary.

8. _____ it _____ by May 28.

---

③ PHRASAL VERBS AND OBJECT PRONOUNS

*Complete these conversations between roommates. Use phrasal verbs
and pronouns.*

1. **A:** I haven't picked up the list of topics for our science paper yet.

   B: I'll _____pick it up_____ for you. I'm going to the science office this

   afternoon.

2. **A:** Hey, guys. We've really got to clean up the kitchen. It's a mess.

   B: It's my turn to _____. I'll do it after dinner.

3. **A:** Did you remember to call your mom up?

   B: Oops! I'll _____ tonight.

4. A: Hey. Can you turn down that music? I'm trying to concentrate.

   B: Sorry. I'll _____ right away.

5. A: It's after 9:00. Do you think we should wake John up?

   B: Don't _____. He said he wanted to sleep late.

6. A: Professor Cho turned down my science topic.

   B: Really? Why did she _____?

7. A: When do we have to hand in our reports?

   B: We have to _____ by Friday.

8. A: I wanted to drop off my report this afternoon, but I'm not going to have time.

   B: I can _____ for you. I have an appointment with

   Professor Cho at noon.

④ WORD ORDER

Professor Cho made a list of things to do with her class. Unscramble the words to make sentences. In some cases, more than one answer is possible.

1. sit / with the class / down _____ Sit down with the class. _____

2. the homework problems / up / bring _____

3. out / common mistakes / point _____

4. them / over / talk _____

5. go / to the next unit / on _____

6. Friday's class / off / call _____

7. up / the final exam questions / make _____

8. them / out / hand _____

5 EDITING

Read this student's letter. Find and correct eleven mistakes in the use of phrasal verbs. The first mistake is already corrected.

Dear Katy,

How are things going? I'm already into the second month of the spring semester, and I've got a lot of work to do. For science class, I have to write a term paper. The
                              up
professor made ~~over~~ a list of possible topics. After looking over them, I think I've

picked one out. I'm going to write about chimpanzees. I've already gone to the library

to look some information about them in the encyclopedia up. I found up some very

interesting facts.

Did you know that their hands look very much like their feet, and that they have

fingernails and toenails? Their thumbs and big toes are "opposable." This makes it

easy for them to pick things out with both their fingers and toes. Their arms are longer

than their legs. This helps out them, too, because they can reach out to fruit growing

on thin branches that could not otherwise support their weight. Adult males weigh

between 90 and 115 pounds, and they are about four feet high when they stand out.

Like humans, chimpanzees are very social. They travel in groups called

"communities." Mothers bring out their chimps, who stay with them until about the

age of seven. Even after the chimps have grown up, there is still a lot of contact with

other chimpanzees.

I could go on, but I need to stop writing now so I can clean out my room (it's a

mess!) a little before going to bed. It's late already, and I have to get early up tomorrow

morning for my 9:00 a.m. class.

Please write and let me know how you are. Or call up me

sometime! It would be great to speak to you.

Best,

Tony

UNIT

11

ABILITY:
CAN, COULD, BE ABLE TO

1 AFFIRMATIVE AND NEGATIVE STATEMENTS WITH CAN AND COULD

Read about this student's ability in English. Then complete the statements for each item.

Student's Name *Fernando Ochoa*

English Language Ability Questionnaire

Skill	Now	Before This Course
1. understand conversational English	✓	✗
2. understand recorded announcements	✗	✗
3. read an English newspaper	✓	✓
4. read an English novel	✗	✗
5. speak on the phone	✓	✗
6. speak with a group of people	✓	✗
7. write a social letter	✓	✗
8. write a business letter	✗	✗
9. order a meal in English	✓	✓
10. go shopping	✓	✓

1. Before this course he ___couldn't understand conversational English.___

   Now ___he can understand conversational English.___

2. He ___couldn't understand recorded announcements___ before the course,

   and he still ___can't understand them.___

(continued on next page)

3. He _____ now, and he _____

before, too.

4. He _____ before the course, and he still _____.

5. Now he _____, but before the course he_____.

6. Before the course, he _____, but now he _____.

7. Before the course, he _____. Now he_____.

8. _____

9. _____

10. _____

SUMMARY: Fernando _____ do a lot more now than he

_____ before the course.

2 QUESTIONS AND ANSWERS WITH *CAN* AND *COULD*

Complete this interview with another student.

1. (speak / any other languages?)

 A: _Can you speak any other languages?_ _____

 B: ____Yes, I can.____ I speak two other languages.

2. (What / languages / speak?)

 A: _____

 B: Spanish and French.

3. (speak Spanish / when you were a child?)

 A: _____

 B: _____ I learned it as an adult.

4. (speak French?)

 A: _____

 B: _____ We spoke French some of the time at home.

5. (Before you came here / understand spoken English?)

   A: _____

   B: _____ I didn't understand anything!

6. What about now? (understand song lyrics?)

   A: _____

   B: _____ Especially if I listen to them more than once.

7. (Before this course / write a business letter in English?)

   A: _____

   B: _____ But I used to write in English to my friends.

8. Enough about languages. Tell me some more about yourself. For example,

   (drive a car before you came here?)

   A: _____

   B: _____ I was too young.

9. (drive a car now?)

   A: _____

   B: _____ I still haven't learned.

10. (swim?) We're not too far from the beach here.

    A: _____

    B: _____ I've been swimming since I was a little kid.

11. What about surfing? (surf before you came here?)

    A: _____

    B: _____ But I learned to surf the first month I was here.

12. (What / do now / that / not do before?)

    A: _____

    B: Oh! I _____ a lot of things now that I

    _____ before.

3 AFFIRMATIVE AND NEGATIVE STATEMENTS WITH *BE ABLE TO*

Complete this article about hearing loss. Use the correct form of **be able to** *and the verbs in parentheses ( ).*

There are more than 26 million people in the United States who have some degree of hearing loss. There are two major types of hearing loss.

1. **Sound Sensitivity Loss.** People with this kind of loss _____ <u>are not able to hear</u> _____

   1. (not hear)

   soft sounds—a whisper or a bird singing, for example. However, when sounds are

   loud enough, they _____ them correctly.

   2. (interpret)

2. **Sound Discrimination Loss.** People with this kind of hearing loss

   _____ one sound from another. As a result of this, they

   3. (not distinguish)

   _____ speech—even when it is loud enough for them to

   4. (not understand)

   hear.

   How do people with hearing disabilities cope in a hearing world? Most people with

   hearing impairments _____ some sounds. Since the

   5. (hear)

   widespread availability of the hearing aid, many people

   _____ some of their ability to hear. Some people with

   6. (regain)

   hearing disabilities _____ lips. But, at best, lip reading is

   7. (read)

   only 30 to 50 percent effective. Even a good lip reader _____

   8. (not recognize)

   all the sounds. Just ask someone to silently mouth the words *pat, bat,* and *mat.* They

   sound different, but they all *look* the same. Besides, the human eye

   _____ fast enough to process speech by vision alone. By

   9. (not work)

   far the most successful form of communication is signing—the use of sign language.

   People with hearing impairments _____ successfully with

   10. (communicate)

   others who know this language.

4 **QUESTIONS AND SHORT ANSWERS WITH *BE ABLE TO***

Sensitivity to sound is measured in decibels. Look at this chart. It shows the decibel measurements of some common sounds.

0 decibels	softest sound a typical ear can hear
20 decibels	a whisper
45 decibels	soft conversational speech
55 decibels	loud conversational speech
65 decibels	loud music from the radio
75 decibels	city traffic
100 decibels	loud factory noise
110 decibels	loud amplified rock band
120 decibels	loud power tool
140 decibels	jet engine at takeoff

Source: Rezen and Hausman, *Coping with Hearing Loss: A Guide for Adults and Their Families*, New York: Dembner Books, 1985.

Mary has a hearing loss of 50 decibels. This means she will not be able to hear sounds that have a loudness of 50 decibels or less. Ask and answer these questions about what Mary will be able to hear at the party she is going to.

1. **A:** _____Will she be able to hear_____ a whisper?

   B: _____No, she won't._____

2. **A:** _____ loud music?

   B: _____

3. **A:** _____ a soft conversation?

   B: _____

4. **A:** _____ loud traffic?

   B: _____

5. **A:** _____ a loud conversation?

   B: _____

5 CONTRAST: *CAN* AND *BE ABLE TO*

Read this information about a well-known actress who is deaf.
Complete it with the correct form of **can** *or* **be able to** *and the verbs in*
parentheses ( ). Use **can** *or* **could** *when possible.*

Actress Marlee Matlin _____*could hear*_____ at
                                   1. (hear)
birth but lost her hearing at the age of 18 months as a result

of a childhood illness. By the age of five, she

_____ lips. Shortly after that, she
          2. (read)

mastered sign language. At first, Matlin felt angry and

frightened by her hearing impairment. "I wanted to be perfect,

and I _____ my deafness," she said during an interview. With
          3. (not accept)

time, however, she _____ to accept it.
                          4. (learn)

Matlin began her acting career at the age of eight, when she performed in theater for the

deaf. In 1986, she received an Oscar nomination for best actress in the Hollywood film,

Children of a Lesser God. In the movie she played the role of an angry woman who was

deaf and did not want to speak. For Matlin, however, speaking is very important. At the

Oscar ceremonies, she _____ her award verbally. It was the first time
                              5. (accept)

the public heard her speak. "It's what I wanted to do, because a lot of people all over the

world _____ me for who I am," she said. Matlin was worried however.
          6. (see)

"What other roles _____ I _____ in the future?"
                                                          7. (do)

she asked.

Since her Oscar award, Matlin has appeared in another Hollywood movie, a television

movie, and has co-starred in her own TV series. One reviewer said about Matlin, "She

_____ more saying nothing than most people
          8. (do)

_____ talking." Matlin doesn't think of herself as a "deaf actress."
          9. (do)

She is an "actress who happens to be deaf." She _____ both the deaf
                                                         10. (master)

and hearing worlds. Since recent intensive speech training, she _____
                                                                       11. (speak)

very clearly, and in the future, she hopes she _____ roles that are not
                                                       12. (get)

specifically written for people with hearing impairments.

6 EDITING

Read this student's composition. Find and correct seven mistakes in the
use of **can** *and* **be able to**. *The first mistake is already corrected.*

---

                                   couldn't

Before I came to this country I ~~can't~~ do many things in English. For example, I

couldn't follow a conversation if many people were talking at the same time. I

remember one occasion at a party. I wasn't able understand a word! I felt so

uncomfortable. Finally, my aunt came to pick me up, and I could leave the party.

    Today I can to understand much better. Since last month I can practice a lot. I

am taking classes at the adult center. My teacher is very good. She can explains

things well, and she always gives us the chance to talk a lot in class. I can do a lot

now, and I think in a few more months I can do even more.

---

7 PERSONALIZATION

Look at the English Language Ability Questionnaire in Exercise 1. Write
sentences about your English ability now and before this course.

1. _____

_____

2. _____

_____

3. _____

_____

4. _____

_____

PERMISSION: MAY, COULD, CAN, DO YOU MIND IF . . . ?

 QUESTIONS AND RESPONSES

Match these classroom questions and responses.

Questions

1. __d__ Do you mind if I bring my friends to class?

2. _____ May I ask a question?

3. _____ Do you mind if I tape the lesson?

4. _____ Could I open the window?

5. _____ Can we review Unit 4?

6. _____ May I leave the room?

7. _____ Could we use our dictionaries?

8. _____ Could I borrow a pen?

Responses

a. Certainly. The key to the rest room is hanging on the wall.

b. Not at all.

c. Sure. I hope I can answer it.

d. Actually, I do mind. It's already pretty crowded.

e. Sure. But remember, you don't have to look up every word.

f. I'm afraid we can't. We're running out of time.

g. Sure. But please remember to return it.

h. Go right ahead. It's quite warm in here.

2 QUESTIONS

Read the situations. Complete the questions.

1. You want to open the window.

   May ___I open the window?_____

2. Your whole class wants to review Unit 6.

   Could _____

3. You want to borrow a classmate's pen.

Can _____

4. You want to look at someone's class notes.

Do you mind if _____

5. You want to come late to the next class.

Do you mind if _____

6. Your husband wants to come to the next class with you.

Could _____

7. You want to ask a question.

May _____

8. You and a classmate would like to use a dictionary.

Can _____

9. You and your classmates want to leave five minutes early.

Could _____

10. Your sister wants to go on the class trip with the rest of the class.

Do you mind if _____

③ PERSONALIZATION

Imagine that you are in class. Read the following situations. Ask your teacher for permission to do something.

1. You don't understand something the teacher is saying.

_____

2. You don't feel well.

_____

3. Your cousin from (your country) is going to visit you for a week.

_____

4 AFFIRMATIVE AND NEGATIVE STATEMENTS

Look at the flier. Complete the statements. Use the words in parentheses ( ).

CLASS TRIP

You are invited to our annual class picnic on Sunday,

May 26, at Glenwood State Park.

Food and Beverages Welcome, but

No Glass Containers Please!

Bus Tickets $5.00 (check or cash)

Advance Purchase Only • No Refunds

Bring a Friend!

1. You _____ may bring _____ a friend.
    (may / bring)

2. You _____ your own food.
    (can / bring)

3. You _____ juice from a glass bottle at the picnic.
    (can / drink)

4. You _____ for your bus ticket by check.
    (can / pay)

5. You _____ for your bus ticket by cash.
    (can / pay)

6. You _____ for your ticket by credit card.
    (may / pay)

7. You _____ your bus ticket on the day of the trip.
    (may / purchase)

8. You _____ a refund.
    (can / get)

5 EDITING

*Read this professor's response to an e-mail from one of his students. (The professor's answers are in **bold** print.) Find and correct five mistakes in making and responding to requests. The first mistake is already corrected.*

Subj: missed classes—Reply
Date: 04-22-01   11:22:43 EST
From: aolinsky@bryant.edu
To: Timbotwo@hotline.com

>>>Timbotwo@hotline.com> 04/22/01   9:05am>>>

Professor Olinsky—

I've been sick for the past two days. That's why I missed the last test. May I ~~taking~~ a **take**

make up exam?

Yes. If you bring a doctor's note.

Could my brother comes to class and take notes for me on Tuesday?

Yes, he could.

Do you mind when he tapes the class for me?

Not at all. He's welcome to tape the class.

One last request—I know I missed some handouts. May I have please copies of them?

Sure. I'll give them to your brother on Tuesday.

Thanks a lot.

Tim

REQUESTS:
WILL, WOULD, COULD, CAN,
WOULD YOU MIND . . . ?

1 REQUESTS AND RESPONSES

Match these office requests and responses.

Requests	**Responses**
1. __d__ Could you meet me tomorrow at 8:00 A.M.?	**a.** I'd be glad to. When do you need it?
2. _____ Will you please type this memo for me?	**b.** Sure. It is pretty cold in here.
3. _____ Could you show me how to copy an electronic file?	**c.** Of course I can. When would you like to reschedule it?
4. _____ Would you please spell your last name for me?	**d.** I'm sorry. I have an early morning dentist appointment.
5. _____ Would you mind mailing this letter for me?	**e.** Sure. It's DJohn@iol.com.
6. _____ Can you cancel tomorrow's meeting for me? I have to go out of town.	**f.** Sure. . . . Hello, J and R Equities.
7. _____ Will you shut the window, please?	**g.** Sure. It's M-A-R-D-J-A-I-T.
8. _____ Would you get that box down from the closet?	**h.** Sorry, but I'm not familiar with that software program.
9. _____ Could you get the phone for me?	**i.** I'd like to, but it's too heavy for me to lift.
10. _____ Can you give me Doug Johnson's e-mail address?	**j.** Not at all.

Write the numbers of the requests that were granted: __2,_____

Write the numbers of the requests that were refused: _____

② REQUESTS

These conversations take place in an office. Complete them, using the phrases in the box.

~~answer the phone~~	lend me $5.00
come to my office	mail a letter
explain this note to me	open the window
get Frank's phone number	pick up a sandwich
keep the noise down	stay late tonight

1. **A:** Could you_____*answer the phone*_____? My hands are full.

   B: Sure. I'll get it.

2. **A:** Would you mind _____? It's really hot in here.

   B: No, not at all.

3. **A:** Can you please _____ for me?

   B: Certainly. I pass the post office on my way home.

4. **A:** I'm going to the coffee shop. Can I get you anything?

   B: Could you _____ for me?

5. **A:** Would you mind _____? I really have to get this report

   done by tomorrow.

   B: I'm sorry, but I have to visit my aunt in the hospital.

6. **A:** Will you _____, please? I can't hear myself think!

   B: Sorry!

7. **A:** Can you _____ when you have the chance?

   B: Sure. I'll be right there.

8. **A:** Would you _____ for me?

   B: It's 555-4345.

9. **A:** Would you mind _____?

   B: Not at all. What is it that you don't understand?

10. **A:** Could you _____?

    B: Oh, I'm sorry. I'm short on cash.

(continued on next page)

❸ EDITING

Read these office notes. Find and correct six mistakes in the use of requests. The first mistake is already corrected.

1.

Meng,

Would you ~~tiled~~ file these, please?

Thanks.

R.L.

2.

write it down

Hi Ted,

Could you please remember to turn off the lights when you leave?

Thanks,

Lynn

3.

HANK.
WILL YOU RETURN PLEASE THE STAPLER?

BRAD

4.

Melida,

Can you make 5 copies of these pages, please?
Thanks.

Ellen

5.

John,

Would you mind leave the finished report on my desk?

Roy

6.

Celia,
Could you please remember to lock the door.
Thank you.

Diana

7.

> *Would you please to call Ms. Rivera before the end of the day?*
>
> *Thanks,*
> *JF*

8.

> *Could you print out 10 copies of the Hendricks report?*
> *Also, would you mind to e-mail Lisa Barker a copy?*
>
> *Thanks a lot.*
> *Heather*

4 PERSONALIZATION

Write one request that you would like to make of each of the following people.

1. (To your teacher) _____

2. (To a classmate) _____

3. (To a friend) _____

4. (To your boss) _____

5. (To your landlord) _____

6. (To _____) _____

ADVICE:
SHOULD, OUGHT TO,
HAD BETTER

 QUESTIONS AND ANSWERS WITH *SHOULD*

Read this invitation. Use the information in the invitation to complete the phone conversation.

YOU ARE INVITED TO A PARTY!

FOR: *Scott's SURPRISE graduation barbecue*

DATE: *June 11*

TIME: *2:00 P.M. sharp!*

PLACE: *20 Greenport Avenue*

RSVP by May 15. Please don't call here!

Leave a message at 555-3234.

No Gifts, please!

(but please bring something to drink)

WANDA: Hi, Tania.

TANIA: Hi, Wanda. What's up?

WANDA: Aunt Rosa's having a graduation party for Scott. She didn't have
your new address, so she asked me to call and invite you. It's on
June 11. Can you come?

TANIA: Sure. Just give me all the information. (What time / be there?)

_____What time should I be there?_____
                                                        1.

WANDA: Let's see. I have the invitation right here.

_____You should be there at 2:00 P.M. sharp._____
                                                        2.

TANIA: (What / wear?)

_____
                                                        3.

WANDA: Something casual. It's a barbecue.

TANIA: (bring a gift?)

_____
                                                        4.

WANDA: _____ The invitation says "no gifts."
                    5.

TANIA: OK. What about food? (bring something to eat or drink?)

_____
                                                        6.

WANDA: _____
                                                        7.

Oh, and the invitation says "RSVP." In other words, Aunt Rosa wants a response.

TANIA: (When / I respond?)

_____
                                                        8.

WANDA: _____
                                                        9.

TANIA: (call Aunt Rosa?)

_____
                                                        10.

WANDA: _____ I forgot to tell you. It's a surprise party!
                    11.

TANIA: OK. (Who / call?)

_____
                                                        12.

WANDA: _____
                                                        13.

TANIA: Fine. Sounds like fun. I'll see you there. Thanks for calling.

WANDA: No problem. See you there.

2 AFFIRMATIVE AND NEGATIVE STATEMENTS WITH *HAD BETTER*

Friends are giving Scott advice about looking for a job. Complete the advice. Use **had better** *or* **had better not** *and the appropriate verbs from the box.*

arrive	can	dress	have	~~look at~~	tell	write
ask	chew	go	leave	stare	thank	

1. _____You'd better look at_____ the newspaper want ads every day.

2. _____ everyone you know that you are looking for a job. "Networking" is one of the best ways to find employment.

3. _____ your old job before you find a new one. That way you'll always have some money coming in.

4. _____ late for a job interview.

5. _____ a good resume.

6. _____ nicely when you go on an interview. Don't wear your jeans!

7. _____ gum during an interview.

8. _____ call the interviewer by his or her first name. Use *Mr.* or *Ms.* unless the interviewer tells you that it is OK to be less formal.

9. _____ at the floor! Remember to make eye contact with the interviewer.

10. _____ for too much money right away. You can always get a raise after you begin.

11. _____ the interviewer at the end of the interview.

12. _____ on a lot of interviews. It's good practice.

13. _____ a lot of patience. It can take a long time.

3 **QUESTIONS AND ANSWERS:** *SHOULD, OUGHT TO,* **AND** *HAD BETTER*

Scott is getting ready for a job interview. Complete his conversation with a friend. Use **should**, **ought to**, *and* **had better**. *Sometimes more than one answer is possible.*

SCOTT: _____ Should I wear _____ my green suit?
1. (wear)

DENNIS: I don't think so. I think _____ your navy blue one. It's
2. (wear)

more conservative.

SCOTT: _____ my boss about the interview?
3. (tell)

DENNIS: No. _____ until you get a job before you say anything
4. (wait)

to your old boss.

SCOTT: I think we're going out for lunch after the interview.

_____ to pay?
5. (offer)

DENNIS: I don't think so. _____ for your lunch. The interviewer
6. (pay)

usually does that.

SCOTT: _____ a thank-you note after the interview?
7. (write)

DENNIS: That's always a good idea.

SCOTT: When _____ it?
8. (send)

DENNIS: _____ a few days. That way you can always include
9. (wait)

something you forgot to say during the interview.

SCOTT: Well, _____ to say anything important!
10. (not forget)

DENNIS: Try to relax. I'm sure you'll do fine.

SCOTT: I hope so. _____ you after the interview?
11. (call)

DENNIS: _____ me or I'll never speak to you again!
12. (call)

4 EDITING

Read this letter. Find and correct five mistakes in the use of modals giving advice. The first mistake is already corrected.

Dear Scott,

Congratulations on your graduation! Your aunt and I are very proud of you.

I hear you are looking for a job. You know, you really ought to OR should ~~oughta~~ speak to your cousin Mike. He's had a lot of experience in this area. You shouldn't taking the first job they offer you. You've better give yourself a lot of time to find something you'll enjoy. It's important to be happy with what you do.

Maybe you should speak to a job counselor. In any case, you oughtn't rush into anything! Should I ask Mike to call you? He really should gets in touch with you about this.

Well, that's enough advice for one letter.

All my love,

Uncle Ed

5 PERSONALIZATION

A friend of yours is very unhappy at his or her job. Give your friend some advice.

1. _____

2. _____

3. _____

4. _____

5. _____

SUGGESTIONS:
LET'S, COULD, WHY DON'T . . . ?,
WHY NOT . . . ?,
HOW ABOUT . . . ?

1 SUGGESTIONS

*Match the two halves of each suggestion. Notice the
end punctuation—period (.) or question mark (?).*

1. __c__ My feet hurt. Why don't we   **a.** going to a movie?

2. _____ The weather's terrible. How about   **b.** have a cup of coffee.

3. _____ We have an hour before the show starts. We could   **c.** take a taxi?

4. _____ You look exhausted. Why don't I   **d.** go to the beach.

5. _____ This concert is terrible. Let's not   **e.** getting a slice of pizza?

6. _____ I'm really hungry. How about   **f.** change hotels?

7. _____ There's so much to see! How about   **g.** meet you back at the hotel?

8. _____ If John's unhappy at the Blue Water Inn, why doesn't he   **h.** buy some souvenirs there.

9. _____ It's going to be hot tomorrow. Let's   **i.** taking a walking tour?

10. _____ There's a gift shop. Maybe we could   **j.** stay until the end.

2 PUNCTUATION

Circle the correct phrase in italics to complete these conversations
between tourists on vacation. Add the correct punctuation—period (.) or
question mark (?).

1. **A:** I'm exhausted. We've been walking for hours.

    B: How about / <u>Why don't we</u> sit on that bench for a while __?__

2. **A:** I'm almost out of film.

    B: There's a drugstore over there. <u>Maybe you could / Let's not</u> get film there _____

3. **A:** It would be nice to see some of the countryside.

    B: <u>Let's / How about</u> rent a car _____

4. **A:** <u>Why not / How about</u> taking a bus tour _____

    B: That's a good idea. It's less expensive than renting a car.

5. **A:** I want to take a picture of that building. <u>Why don't you / How about</u> stand in front

    of it _____

    B: OK.

6. **A:** We have an hour before we have to meet the rest of our tour group.

    B: <u>Let's / Let's not</u> get a cup of coffee in that cafe _____

    A: Good idea. I could use something to drink.

7. **A:** I heard it's going to rain tomorrow.

    B: <u>Maybe we could / How about</u> go to a museum _____

8. **A:** I really need to get a better map of the city.

    B: <u>Why don't you / Let's not</u> stop at that tourist information office _____

    I'm sure they have maps.

9. **A:** I don't know what to get for my daughter.

    B: <u>Why don't you / How about</u> getting one of those sweatshirts _____

10. **A:** Look at that beautiful building. Why don't you take a picture of it?

    B: <u>That's a good idea / Because I don't want to</u> _____

③ SUGGESTIONS

Look at the tourist information. Complete the conversation. Use the
suggestions in the pamphlet.

BOSTON Highlights

Here are some of the many things you can do in this "capital of New England":

❏ **Go to Haymarket**—open-air fruit and vegetable stands (Fridays and Saturdays only).

☑ **Visit Faneuil Hall Marketplace**—restoration of Boston's historic Quincy Market. Shops, restaurants.

❏ **Go to The New England Aquarium**—412 species, 7,606 specimens.

❏ **Walk along the waterfront**—offices, shops, parks for picnics.

❏ **Take the "T"**—Boston's subway system.

❏ **Take a boat excursion**—cruise the harbor and Massachusetts Bay (1¹/₂ hours).

❏ **Go shopping in Downtown Crossing**—Boston's pedestrian zone.

❏ **Take an elevator to the top of the John Hancock Observatory**—the tallest building in New England.

❏ **Walk the Freedom Trail**—1¹/₂ miles of historic points of interest.

❏ **Eat at Legal Seafoods**—restaurant chain famous for fresh fish at reasonable prices. (No reservations accepted.)

A: Wow, there's so much to do! I don't know where to begin!

B: Why don't we ___visit Faneuil Hall Marketplace___? We can have breakfast there and then
  1.
do some shopping.

A: Sounds good. How will we get there?

B: Let's _____. I always like to see what the public
  2.
transportation is like.

(continued on next page)

A: OK. After Faneuil Hall, maybe we could _____ and pick up

  some fresh fruit for later on. It's right across from there.
  _{3.}

B: We can't. It's only open Fridays and Saturdays.

A: Oh, too bad. How about _____? We could get a "bird's-eye"

  view of the city that way.
  _{4.}

B: I don't know. I'm a little afraid of heights. But I've got another idea. Why don't we

  _____? That way we could still see a lot of the city.
  _{5.}

A: Fine. It'll be nice being on the water. And afterwards, how about

  _____? I hear they have the largest glass-enclosed saltwater
  _{6.}

  tank in the world.

B: Speaking of fish, why don't we _____ tonight?
  _{7.}

A: OK. But we'll have to go early if we don't want to wait. They don't take reservations.

B: That's no problem.

A: So we've decided what to do for breakfast and dinner. What about lunch?

B: Maybe we could _____ and have a picnic in the park. And
  _{8.}

  then, how about _____? I need to buy some souvenirs, and
  _{9.}

  we won't have to worry about traffic. It's a pedestrian zone.

A: I don't know. Why don't we _____? I'd really like to see some
  _{10.}

  more historic sights. We can look for souvenirs tomorrow.

---

4 PERSONALIZATION

*Imagine you are in Boston. Look at the flier in Exercise 3. Complete
these suggestions to a friend.*

1. Why don't we _____

2. How about _____

3. Let's _____

4. Maybe we could _____

5. But let's not _____

UNIT

PRESENT PERFECT:
SINCE AND *FOR*

1 SPELLING: REGULAR AND IRREGULAR VERBS

Write the past participles.

Base Form	Simple Past	Past Participle
1. be	was/were	been
2. look	looked	_____
3. come	came	_____
4. bring	brought	_____
5. play	played	_____
6. have	had	_____
7. get	got	_____
8. fall	fell	_____
9. watch	watched	_____
10. lose	lost	_____
11. win	won	_____
12. eat	ate	_____

2 SINCE OR FOR

Put these time expressions in the correct column.

~~1993~~	4:00 P.M.	Monday	a day	yesterday
an hour	she was a child	a long time	ten years	many months

Since	For
1993	_____
_____	_____
_____	_____
_____	_____

3 AFFIRMATIVE STATEMENTS WITH *SINCE* AND *FOR*

Complete these brief biographies of two people who have been famous since they were children. Use the present perfect form of the verbs in parentheses ( ) and choose between **since** *and* **for**.

1. Tiger Woods (1976–   ) When Tiger Woods was only eighteen

months old, his father gave him a sawed-off golf club. Woods

_____<u>has loved</u>_____ the game of golf
       1. (love)

_____ then. As a teenager, he won
     2. (since / for)

many amateur titles. At sixteen he was the youngest person to

play in a professional golf tournament.

_____ then he _____ to win many
   3. (Since / For)   **4. (go on)**

major tournaments and to break many records. _____ the past
                       5. (Since / For)

few years, TV viewers _____ him in many commercials.
         6. (see)

_____ he turned professional, Woods
   7. (Since / For)

_____ more money and _____
   8. (earn)   **9. (break)**

more records at a younger age than any other golfer.

2. Jodie Foster (1962–   ) Jodie Foster

_____ an actress
         1. (be)

_____ most of her life. At the age of
     2. (since / for)

three, she began appearing in television commercials. She made

her first movie in 1972 and _____ in
              3. (appear)

dozens of movies _____ then. In
          4. (since / for)

1985, she graduated with honors from Yale University. _____
                 5. (Since / For)

her graduation, she _____ two Oscars for Best Actress, for her
      6. (receive)

roles in *The Accused* and *The Silence of the Lambs*, she _____
                             7. (direct)

her first film, *Little Man Tate*, and she _____ her own
            8. (form)

production company. _____ 1998, Foster
      9. (Since / For)

_____ a new role—that of a mother to son Charles, born on
   10. (take on)

July 20.

4 QUESTIONS AND ANSWERS

Ask and answer questions about the people in Exercise 3.

Biography 1

1. How long / Tiger Woods / love golf?

   A: _How long has Tiger Woods loved golf?_

   B: _He has loved golf since he was eighteen months old._

   OR

   He has loved golf for more than twenty years.

2. How long / he / be a professional golfer?

   A: _____

   B: _____

3. he / win any major tournaments since he turned professional?

   A: _____

   B: _____

4. How long / he / be in TV commercials?

   A: _____

   B: _____

Biography 2

5. How long / Jodie Foster / be an actress?

   A: _____

   B: _____

6. she / win any Oscars since 1985?

   A: _____

   B: _____

7. she / direct any movies since she graduated from Yale?

   A: _____

   B: _____

8. How long / she / be a mother?

   A: _____

   B: _____

⑤ AFFIRMATIVE AND NEGATIVE STATEMENTS

Read the pairs of sentences (a. and b.). Write a summary sentence that has a meaning similar to the two sentences.

1. a. Carlos became a tennis player in 1979.
  b. He is still a tennis player.

SUMMARY: <u>Carlos has been a tennis player since 1979.</u>

2. a. Fei-Mei and Natasha competed in 1992.
  b. That was the last time they competed.

SUMMARY: <u>Fei-Mei and Natasha haven't competed since 1992.</u>

3. a. Min Ho won two awards in 1998.
  b. He won another award in 1999.

SUMMARY: _____ since 1997.

4. a. Marilyn appeared in a movie in 1998.
  b. She appeared in another movie last year.

SUMMARY: _____ since 1997.

5. a. Victor and Marilyn saw each other in 1998.
  b. That was the last time they saw each other.

SUMMARY: _____

6. a. Andreas lost two games in February of this year.
  b. He lost another game last week.

SUMMARY: _____ since February of this year.

7. a. Tanya and Boris became skaters in 1998.
  b. They are still skaters.

SUMMARY: _____ since 1998.

PRESENT PERFECT:
ALREADY AND YET

1 SPELLING: REGULAR AND IRREGULAR VERBS

Write the past participles.

Base Form	Simple Past	Past Participle
1. become	became	become
2. act	acted	_____
3. give	gave	_____
4. keep	kept	_____
5. hold	held	_____
6. travel	traveled	_____
7. sing	sang	_____
8. dance	danced	_____
9. fight	fought	_____
10. know	knew	_____
11. drink	drank	_____
12. smile	smiled	_____

2 QUESTIONS AND STATEMENTS WITH *ALREADY* AND *YET*

Complete these conversations with the correct form of the verbs in parentheses and **already** *or* **yet**.

1. **A:** ____Have____ you ____read____ the paper ____yet____?
         (read)
   B: No. I _____ time _____.
         (have)

2. **A:** They expect a lot of cases of the flu this year.

   B: I _____ a vaccination. I went to
         (get)
   the doctor last week. What about you?

   A: I _____ whether I'm going to get a flu shot.
         (decide)

(continued on next page)

3. A: _____ you _____? I'm really hungry. Maybe we

(eat)

could get a couple of slices of pizza.

B: Sorry. I'd like to, but I _____ dinner.

(have)

---

③ QUESTIONS AND STATEMENTS WITH *ALREADY* AND *YET*

Monica Clarke is a home health aide. Read her list of things to do. She has checked (✓) all the things she's already done. Ask and answer questions about the words in parentheses ( ).

> ### Monday, March 29
>
> ☑ make breakfast for pt.
> ❑ make lunch for pt.
> ☑ take pt.'s temperature
> ❑ give pt. a bath
> ☑ change pt.'s bandages
> ☑ go food shopping
> ❑ do the laundry
> ❑ call doctor for the blood-test results
> ❑ exercise pt.'s legs
> ☑ give pt. medication

1. (breakfast) __Has she made breakfast for the patient yet?__

__She's already made breakfast for the patient.__

2. (lunch) __Has she made lunch for the patient yet?__

__She hasn't made lunch for the patient yet.__

3. (food shopping) _____

_____

4. (medication) _____

_____

5. (doctor) _____

_____

6. (bandages) _____

_____

7. (bath) _____

_____

8. (temperature) _____

_____

9. (laundry) _____

_____

10. (legs) _____

_____

4 EDITING

Read Monica's letter to a friend. Find and correct five mistakes in the use of the present perfect with **already** *and* **yet**. *The first mistake is already corrected.*

> Dear Suzanne,
>
>   It's 8:00 P.M. and I'm exhausted. I'm at my new job. I've already ~~work~~ worked here for two weeks. The job is hard, but I feel that the patient have already made progress. She hasn't walked already, but she's already sat up by herself. She can feed herself now, too. Already she has gained three pounds.
>
>   How are you? When are you coming to visit? Have you decide yet? Please write.
>
>   Love,
>   Monica

UNIT

18 PRESENT PERFECT: INDEFINITE PAST

1 SPELLING: REGULAR AND IRREGULAR VERBS

Write the past participle.

Base Form	Simple Past	Past Participle
1. work	worked	worked
2. begin	began	_____
3. forgive	forgave	_____
4. promise	promised	_____
5. go	went	_____
6. feel	felt	_____
7. grow	grew	_____
8. hear	heard	_____
9. see	saw	_____
10. decide	decided	_____
11. keep	kept	_____
12. act	acted	_____

2 AFFIRMATIVE STATEMENTS

Complete these statements. Use the present perfect form of the correct verbs from Exercise 1.

1. Juliana _____has worked_____ very hard this year.

2. She _____ in two Hollywood movies.

3. We _____ her face on many magazine covers.

4. People _____ to recognize her on the street.

5. I _____ that she is going to star in a new movie.

6. I _____ always _____ that she's a great actress.

7. Even though she is famous, she _____ her life very private.

8. Juliana _____ the press, however, to give an interview if she wins an

Oscar.

3 AFFIRMATIVE AND NEGATIVE STATEMENTS

Every year Hollywood gives out awards for movie achievements. Complete this editorial about the Academy Awards. Use the present perfect form of the verbs in parentheses ( ).

> It's Oscar night once again. You and a billion other people from ninety countries around the
>
> world _____*have*_____ just _____*turned on*_____ your TVs to see who Hollywood will honor
>   **1. (turn on)**
> this year. The Academy of Motion Picture Arts and Sciences _____ nominees to
>   **2. (choose)**
> compete in categories including Best Picture, Best Actor, Best Actress, and Best Director. Actors
>
> and actresses from around the world _____ to Hollywood to take part in the gala
>   **3. (come)**
> event.
>
>   As always, opinions about the nominations _____ mixed. Many groups are
>   **4. (be)**
> unhappy. Lately, there _____ many great roles for women. In fact, there
>   **5. (not be)**
> _____ seldom _____ a Hollywood actress who _____ past
>   **6. (be)**   **7. (work)**
> the age of 45. "I _____ recently _____ several scripts," said one
>   **8. (read)**
> well-known actress, "and I _____ all of them. The stories are ridiculous." This
>   **9. (reject)**
> absence of good roles for women may partly explain why out of more than 2,000 Oscar awards,
>
> fewer than 300 _____ to women.
>   **10. (go)**
>   African-American actors and actresses _____ also _____ excluded.
>   **11. (feel)**
> Fewer than ten _____ awards for acting.
>   **12. (get)**
>   Actors and actresses with physical disabilities _____ major roles either. Many
>   **13. (not get)**
> movies _____ recently _____ the stories of people who are blind or
>   **14. (tell)**
> paralyzed, but "able-bodied" Hollywood stars _____ these parts.
>   **15. (play)**

(continued on next page)

On screen as well as off, we still have a long way to go toward equal opportunity. In the

meantime, Hollywood _____ another evening of glitter and glamour as movies
       16. (produce)
continue to fascinate and entertain us. As one actor said, "They take us to places we

_____ never _____ and allow us to see things we _____
                17. (be)
never _____."
    18. (see)
So, relax, have some popcorn, and enjoy the show.

④ QUESTIONS

Bob Waters is interviewing a movie star. Read the star's answers. Write Bob's questions.

1. **BOB:** How many movies have you been in?

    STAR: I've been in ten movies.

2. **BOB:** _____

    STAR: I've received four nominations for Best Actor.

3. **BOB:** Some actors don't like to see their own films.

    _____

    STAR: No, I haven't. I've never watched the completed films.

4. **BOB:** _____

    STAR: No, never. I've never gone to the Academy Awards. I prefer to watch the event on

    TV.

5. **BOB:** Your last movie was an Italian production.

    _____

    STAR: I've acted in foreign films three times.

6. BOB: _____

    STAR: Yes, I have. I worked with Sophia Loren once.

7. BOB: _____

    STAR: No. I've never been in a French film.

8. BOB: You've made a lot of money in a very short time.

    _____

    STAR: How? It's changed my life in many ways. I've traveled more, I've bought a new

    house . . .

9. BOB: _____

    STAR: No, I haven't. I haven't read any good scripts lately. But I'm sure a good one will

    come my way soon.

5 PERSONALIZATION

Write about your own experience going to the movies, renting a video,
or watching TV.

1. _____ recently _____.

2. _____ lately.

3. _____ never _____.

4. _____ just _____.

UNIT 19

PRESENT PERFECT AND SIMPLE PAST TENSE

 1 PRESENT PERFECT OR SIMPLE PAST TENSE

Complete the chart about Joe Dorsey, a teacher who is looking for a job.

Last Year	This Year
1. Joe answered twenty employment ads.	_____Joe has answered_____ thirty ads.
2. _____ two job interviews.	Joe has had three job interviews.
3. _____ one job offer.	Joe has gotten three job offers.
4. Joe made $24,000.	_____ the same amount of money.
5. Joe was sick once.	_____ sick twice.
6. _____ well.	Joe has looked tired.
7. _____ a new camera.	Joe has bought a VCR.
8. Joe paid with cash.	_____ by credit card.
9. Joe read five books.	_____ two books.
10. _____ discouraged.	Joe has felt more encouraged.

② PRESENT PERFECT OR SIMPLE PAST TENSE

A journalist is interviewing a woman about marriage. Complete the interview with the correct form of the verbs in parentheses ( ).

INTERVIEWER: How long _____*have*_____ you _____*been*_____ married?

                                              1. (be)

WOMAN: Let's see. We _____ married in 1997, so we _____

                          2. (get)   3. (be)

married for just a few years.

INTERVIEWER: And when _____ you _____ your first child?

                                       4. (have)

WOMAN: Well, I _____ a mother pretty quickly. We _____

                  5. (become)   6. (have)

Stephanie ten months after we _____ married.

                                      7. (be)

INTERVIEWER: You say this isn't your first marriage. How long _____ your first

marriage _____?

                      8. (last)

WOMAN: About two years. We _____ in 1989.

                          9. (divorce)

INTERVIEWER: _____ you _____ any kids?

                            10. (have)

WOMAN: No, we _____.

                  11.

INTERVIEWER: Do you still see your first husband?

WOMAN: Yes. We _____ friends. In fact, I _____ him last week.

                  12. (remain)   13. (see)

He and Joe _____ friends, too.

                  14. (become)

INTERVIEWER: _____ he _____?

                        15. (remarry)

WOMAN: No, he _____.

                16.

INTERVIEWER: In your opinion, why _____ your first marriage _____?

                                                             17. (fail)

WOMAN: I think that we _____ married too young. We _____

                  18. (get)   19. (not know)

each other well enough.

INTERVIEWER: Where _____ you _____ Joe?

                          20. (meet)

WOMAN: In Atlanta. We _____ both students there.

                  21. (be)

INTERVIEWER: And when _____ you _____ to Los Angeles?

                            22. (move)

WOMAN: This year. Los Angeles is the third city we _____ in! Joe teaches

                                           23. (live)

college, and it's hard to find a permanent job these days.

③ PRESENT PERFECT OR SIMPLE PAST TENSE

Read some facts about the changing American family. Complete the statements. Use the correct form of the verbs in the boxes.

begin	change	get	have

The American family ___has changed___ a lot in the past forty years. In the 1960s,
      1.
couples _____ to get married at an older age. They also _____
             2.   **3.**
divorced more frequently than they ever did, and they _____ fewer children.
                                                                              4.

be	create	occur	rise

Age

   In 1960, the average age for marriage for women _____ 20.3 and for men,
                                                                               5.
22.8. Today it _____ to 25.0 for women and 26.8 for men. In the early 1960s,
                     6.
most divorces _____ among couples older than 45. Today people of all ages are
                       7.
getting divorced at a very high rate. This, in part, _____ many single-parent
                                                                              8.
homes.

be	begin	have	increase

Birth Rate

   In the mid-1960s, birth rates _____ to drop. Then, almost 60 percent of
                                              9.
women _____ three or more children by the time they _____ in their
              10.   **11.**
late thirties. These days, 35 percent of women in the same age group have only two
children. In addition, the number of births to older women _____ greatly
_____.
      12.

change	get	reach	stay

Living Arrangements

   Before 1960, most children _____ in their parents' homes until they
                                          13.
_____ married. This pattern _____ since then. Today many single
      14.   **15.**
people live alone. Also affecting living arrangements is the fact that life expectancy
_____ an all-time high of 76.5 years. This means that there are a lot more older
      16.
people, and some of them are moving in with their adult children.

4 EDITING

Read this student's letter to a friend. Find and correct eight mistakes in the use of the present perfect and the simple past tense. The first mistake is already corrected.

Dear Jennifer,

    Last month, I ~~have met~~ met the most wonderful guy. His name is Roger, and he is a student in my night class. He lived here since 1992. Before that he lived in Detroit too, so we have a lot in common. Roger has been married for five years but got divorced last April.

    Roger and I spent a lot of time together. Last week I saw him every night, and this week we've already gotten together three times after class. Monday night we have seen a great movie. Did you see <u>The Purple Room</u>? It's playing at all the theaters.

    We decided to take a trip back to Detroit in the summer. Maybe we can get together? It would be great to see you again. Please let me know if you'll be there.

                Love,

                Diana

P.S. I'm enclosing a photo of Roger that I've taken a few weeks ago.

PRESENT PERFECT PROGRESSIVE

1 AFFIRMATIVE STATEMENTS WITH *SINCE* AND *FOR*

Read the information about a married couple, Pete and Amanda Kelly. Write a sentence that summarizes the information.

1. The year is 2000. Pete and Amanda Kelly moved to New York in 1997. They are still living there.

   They have been living in New York since 1997 OR for three years.

2. Amanda began work at the *Daily News* in 1999. She's still working there.

_____

3. Amanda is writing articles about the homeless. She began a series last month.

_____

4. The number of homeless Americans is increasing. It began to increase steadily in 1980.

_____

5. Pete is working at a homeless shelter. He started last month.

_____

6. Pete went back to school last year. He's studying economics.

_____

7. Amanda and Pete started looking for a new apartment two months ago. They are still looking.

_____

② AFFIRMATIVE AND NEGATIVE STATEMENTS

Complete the statements. Use the present perfect progressive form of the verbs in the box.

eat	rain	run	study	wait
feel	~~rub~~	sleep	try	work

1. Amanda's eyes are red. She <u>'s been rubbing</u> _____ them all morning.

2. She's tired. She _____ well lately.

3. She's losing weight. She _____ much lately.

4. Pete is exhausted too. He _____ all night for a test.

5. Amanda doesn't know many people at the *Daily News*. She

   _____ there very long.

6. She just looked out the window. The street is wet. It _____.

7. Pete is out of breath. He _____.

8. He's only five minutes late. Amanda _____ very long.

9. They're going to look at an apartment. They _____ to find

   one for months.

10. It's very hard to find an apartment in New York. They're often too expensive. Amanda

    and Pete _____ very hopeful.

③ PERSONALIZATION

What have or haven't you been doing? Complete these statements with information about yourself. Use the present perfect progressive.

1. _____ all year.

2. _____ lately.

3. _____ since 2000.

4. _____ for the last half hour.

5. _____

4 **QUESTIONS WITH *HOW LONG***

Look at the picture. Ask questions about the man on the bench, the woman with the dog, the children, the police officer, the two men, and the weather. Begin with **How long** *and use the present perfect progressive.*

1. <u>How long has the man been sitting</u> on the bench?

2. _____ under the tree?

3. _____ the dog?

4. _____ ball?

5. _____ it _____?

6. _____ the bus?

PRESENT PERFECT AND PRESENT PERFECT PROGRESSIVE

① PRESENT PERFECT OR PRESENT PERFECT PROGRESSIVE

Read this information about a famous British businesswoman and environmentalist. Complete it with the present perfect or present perfect progressive form of the verbs in parentheses ( ). If either form is possible, use the present perfect progressive.

In a short period of time, Anita Roddick

_____has become_____ one of the most
    1. (become)
successful businesswomen in the world. She is

the owner of an international chain of stores

that sells soaps, makeup, body lotions, and

creams. For more than twenty years, The Body

Shop _____ products that are
    2. (sell)
"environmentally friendly." They are made mostly of natural products

from renewable sources, and they come in biodegradable, recyclable

containers. In addition, Roddick, who _____ for years
                    3. (fight)
against the practice of animal testing of cosmetics, refuses to use any

animals in the testing of her products.

The first Body Shop opened in Brighton, England, in 1976. Since then,

more than 1,500 stores in more than forty-five countries around the world

_____. Roddick relies on the reputation of her products
    4. (open)
and stores to attract customers. She _____ never

_____ much advertising for her stores. Lately, however,
    5. (do)

(continued on next page)

you *will* see Roddick's face if you turn on your TV. She _____ on
6. (appear)
commercials for the American Express charge card.

Roddick spends almost half of her time traveling. Right now she is "on the road." For
the past several months, she _____ around the world in search of new
7. (travel)
ideas for her body-care products.

Roddick is more than a businesswoman. She _____ several awards,
8. (receive)
including the United Nations Global 500 environmental award. She is also concerned with
human rights, and she _____ a London newspaper that is sold by
9. (start)
homeless people.

Roddick _____ an autobiography called *Body and Soul: Profits with*
10. (write)
Principles. Published in 1991, the book shows how Roddick _____
successfully _____ business with social responsibility.
11. (combine)

② PRESENT PERFECT OR PRESENT PERFECT PROGRESSIVE

*Complete this conversation between two friends. Use the present perfect or present
perfect progressive form of the verbs in parentheses ( ).*

A: Hi. I _____ haven't seen _____ you around lately. How
1. (not see)
_____ you _____?
2. (be)

B: OK, thanks. What about you?

A: Not bad. What _____ you _____?
3. (do)

B: Nothing special. What about you?

A: I _____ a book for this business course I'm taking. It's called
4. (read)
Body and Soul. It's pretty interesting. I can lend it to you when I'm done, if you'd like.

B: Who's it by?

A: Anita Roddick. _____ you ever _____ anything
5. (read)
about her?

B: Yes. I _____ a few articles about her in the paper.
6. (see)

A: _____ you ever _____ any of her
                                    7. (buy)

products?

B: As a matter of fact, I _____ her products for years.
                                    8. (use)

A: Oh. Where do you buy them?

B: A new shop _____ just _____ on
                                    9. (open)

Broadway.

A: Wow, they _____ everywhere, haven't they? I wonder where
                                    10. (open)

the next one is going to be.

---

3 **QUESTIONS: PRESENT PERFECT OR
PRESENT PERFECT PROGRESSIVE**

Use the cues to write questions about Anita Roddick.

1. she / sell / cosmetics for a long time?

    Has she been selling cosmetics for a long time?

2. How much money / her business / make this year?

_____

3. How long / she / travel around the world?

_____

4. How many countries / she / visit?

_____

5. How many copies of her book / she / sell?

_____

6. she / write / any books since *Body and Soul*?

_____

7. she / ever appear on TV?

_____

8. How long / she and her husband / live in England?

_____

4 EDITING

Read this student's journal entry. Find and correct seven mistakes in the use of the present perfect and present perfect progressive. The first mistake is already corrected.

Friday, Sept. 15

It's the second week of the fall semester. I've ~~taken~~ *been taking* a business course with Professor McCarthy. For the past two weeks we've studying people who have been becoming very successful in the world of business. As part of the course, we've been reading books by or about internationally famous businesspeople. For example, I've just been finishing a book by Bill Gates, the CEO of Microsoft, called <u>Business @ The Speed of Thought</u>. It was fascinating. Since then I've read <u>Body and Soul</u> by Anita Roddick, the owner of The Body Shop. I've only been reading about fifty pages of the book so far, but it seems interesting. Although I bought her products ever since one of her stores opened in my neighborhood, I really didn't know much about her.

ADJECTIVES AND ADVERBS

UNIT

22

1 SPELLING

Write the adjectives and adverbs.

Adjectives	Adverbs
1. quick	quickly
2. _____	nicely
3. fast	_____
4. good	_____
5. _____	dangerously
6. beautiful	_____
7. _____	hard
8. safe	_____
9. _____	occasionally
10. _____	happily
11. _____	suddenly
12. careful	_____
13. angry	_____
14. _____	unfortunately

2 WORD ORDER

Emily is telling her friend about her new apartment. Put the words in the correct order to make sentences and complete the conversation.

A: Congratulations! (heard about / I / apartment / new / your).

   1.   I heard about your new apartment. _____

B: Thank you! (news / good / fast / travels)!

   2. _____

(continued on next page)

A: What's it like?

B: (five / rooms / has / it / large),

3. _____

and (building / it's / large / a / very / in).

4. _____

A: How's the rent?

B: (too / it's / bad / not).

5. _____

A: And what about the neighborhood?

B: (seems / quiet / it / pretty).

6. _____

But (landlord / the / very / speaks / loudly).

7. _____

A: How come?

B: (well / doesn't / he / hear).

8. _____

A: Well, that doesn't really matter. (it / decision / was / hard / a)?

9. _____

B: Not really. We liked the apartment, and besides (quickly / had to / we / decide).

10. _____

There were a lot of other people interested in it.

A: Oh, no! Look at the time! (I / leave / now / have to).

11. _____

(luck / with / good / apartment / new / your)!

12. _____

B: Thanks. So long.

❸ ADJECTIVE OR ADVERB

Emily wrote a letter to a friend. Complete the letter. Use the correct form of the words in parentheses ( ).

Dear Lauren,

I'm _____totally_____ exhausted! James and I finished moving into our new
      1. (total)
apartment today. It was a lot of _____ work, but everything worked
                                    2. (hard)
out _____.
      3. (good)
    The apartment looks _____. It's _____
                            4. (nice)   5. (extreme)
_____. The only problem is with the heat. I always feel
6. (comfortable)
_____. We'll have to speak to the landlord about it. He seems
   7. (cold)
_____ _____.
   8. (pretty)   9. (friendly)
    People tell me that the neighborhood is very _____. That's
                                                    10. (safe)
_____ _____ because I get home _____
   11. (real)   12. (important)   13. (late)
from work. I hate it when the streets are _____ _____
                                            14. (complete)   15. (empty)
like they were in our old neighborhood. Shopping is _____, too.
                                                      16. (good)
We can get to all the stores very _____. The bus stop is
                                     17. (easy)
_____ the apartment, and the buses run _____.
18. (near)   19. (frequent)
    Why don't you come for a visit? It would be _____ to see you.
                                                  20. (wonderful)
I haven't seen you since our wedding. Please write.

                                                        Love,
                                                        Emily

4 *-ED* OR *-ING* ADJECTIVES

Emily and James are going to rent a video. Circle the correct adjective form to complete these brief movie reviews from a video guide.

At Home at the Movies

BILLY BUDD   Based on Herman Melville's powerful and (1. fascinated /(fascinating)) novel, this well-acted, well-produced film will leave you (2. disturbed / disturbing).

THE BURNING   There's nothing (3. entertained / entertaining) about this 1981 horror film that takes place in a summer camp. You'll be (4. disgusted / disgusting) by all the blood in this story of revenge.

CHARIOTS OF FIRE   Made in England, this is an (5. inspired / inspiring) story about two Olympic runners. Wonderfully acted.

COMING HOME   Jon Voight plays the role of a (6. paralyzed / paralyzing) war veteran in this (7. moved / moving) drama about the effects of war. Powerful.

THE COMPETITION   Well-acted love story about two pianists who fall in love while competing for the top prize in a concert. You'll be (8. moved / moving). Beautiful music.

FOLLOW ME QUIETLY   A (9. frightened / frightening) thriller about a mentally (10. disturbed / disturbing) man who kills people when it rains. Not for the weak-hearted.

THE GRADUATE   Director Mike Nichols won an Academy Award for this funny, but (11. touched / touching) look at a young man trying to figure out his life after college.

THE GREEN WALL   Mario Robles Godoy's photography is absolutely (12. astonished / astonishing) in this story of a young Peruvian family. In Spanish with English subtitles.

INVASION OF THE BODY SNATCH-ERS   One of the most (13. frightened / frightening) science fiction movies ever made. You won't be (14. bored / boring).

WEST SIDE STORY   No matter how many times you see this classic musical, you will never be (15. disappointed / disappointing). The story, based on Shakespeare's *Romeo and Juliet*, is (16. touched / touching), and the music by Leonard Bernstein is delightful and (17. excited / exciting).

WILBUR AND ORVILLE: THE FIRST TO FLY   This is an (18. entertained / entertaining) biography of the two famous Wright brothers. Good for kids, too. They'll learn a lot without ever being (19. bored / boring).

ADJECTIVES: COMPARATIVES AND EQUATIVES

 SPELLING: REGULAR AND IRREGULAR COMPARATIVES

Write the comparative forms of the adjectives.

Adjective	Comparative
1. slow	*slower*
2. expensive	
3. hot	
4. big	
5. good	
6. difficult	
7. pretty	
8. beautiful	
9. bad	
10. long	
11. far	
12. careful	
13. dangerous	
14. early	
15. terrible	
16. wide	
17. noisy	
18. comfortable	
19. wet	
20. cheap	

2 THE COMPARATIVE FORM

*Complete this conversation between two neighbors who meet in a department store. Use the correct form of the words in parentheses ( ). Use **than** when necessary.*

EMILY: Amy!

AMY: Emily! What are you doing here?

EMILY: I'm trying to buy a microwave oven. Do you know if the small ones are really any

_____worse than_____ the _____ ones?
　　　　1. (bad)　　　　　　　　　　**2. (large)**

AMY: I'm not sure, but I think they're _____. Are you getting
　　　　　　　　　　　　　　　　　　3. (slow)

things for your new apartment?

EMILY: Yes. James and I moved in last Friday.

AMY: How do you like it?

EMILY: It's great. It's _____ our old one. It has an extra
　　　　　　　　　　　4. (big)

bedroom. And it faces the back, so it's _____. You can't
　　　　　　　　　　　　　　　　　　　　　5. (quiet)

hear the traffic at all.

AMY: How's the rent?

EMILY: That's the only problem. It's a little _____.
　　　　　　　　　　　　　　　　　　　　　6. (expensive)

AMY: But it's _____ a house.
　　　　　　7. (cheap)

EMILY: That's true. The location is _____ for us, too. Everything
　　　　　　　　　　　　　　　　8. (good)

is _____—shopping, schools.
　　9. (convenient)

AMY: Isn't it _____ from your office, though?
　　　　　10. (far)

EMILY: Yes. But I take the express bus and get there even _____
　　　　　　　　　　　　　　　　　　　　　　　　　11. (fast)

before. Besides, I can relax on the bus, so it's _____.
　　　　　　　　　　　　　　　　　　　　　　12. (comfortable)

AMY: That's good. Emily, do you know the time?

EMILY: Yes. It's 4:35.

AMY: Oh! It's _____ I thought! I've got to run. Good luck with
　　　　　13. (late)

your new apartment.

EMILY: Thanks! I'll give you a call when we get _____. Maybe we
　　　　　　　　　　　　　　　　　　　　14. (settled)

could have lunch together.

AMY: Sounds great.

3 THE COMPARATIVE FORM

*Look at this chart comparing two microwave ovens. Complete the sentences, using the words in parentheses ( ). Also, fill in the blanks with the brand—**X** or **Y**.*

Brand	Price	Size (cubic ft.)	Weight (lbs.)	Defrosting	Heating	Speed	Noise
X	$181	0.5	31	●	○	◐	○
Y	$147	0.6	36	◐	●	●	◐

1. Brand _____X_____ is _____more expensive than_____ Brand _____Y_____.
   (expensive)

2. Brand _____ is _____ Brand _____.
   (cheap)

3. Brand _____ is _____ Brand _____.
   (large)

4. Brand _____ is _____ Brand _____.
   (heavy)

5. For defrosting food, Brand _____ is _____
   (efficient)
   Brand _____.

6. For heating food, Brand _____ is _____
   (effective)
   Brand _____.

7. Brand _____ is _____ Brand _____.
   (fast)

8. Brand _____ is _____ Brand _____.
   (noisy)

9. In general, Brand _____ seems _____
   (good)
   Brand _____.

10. In general, Brand _____ seems _____
    (bad)
    Brand _____.

4 COMPARISONS WITH *AS . . . AS*

Read the facts about Los Angeles and New York City. Complete the sentences. Use the words in parentheses ( ) with **as . . . as** *or* **not as . . . as**.

	Los Angeles	New York City
Total population	3,555,638	7,380,906
Population per square mile	7,572	23,894
Land area	469.3 square miles	308.9 square miles
Average temperature	57.2°F (January)	31.8°F (January)
	74.1°F (July)	76.7°F (July)
Sunny days	143	107
Annual rainfall	12″	40″
Average wind speed	7.4 mph	9.4 mph

1. In population, Los Angeles is _____ <u>not as big as</u> _____ New York.
   (big)
2. Los Angeles _____ New York.
   (crowded)
3. In land area, New York is _____ Los Angeles.
   (big)
4. In the winter, Los Angeles is _____ New York.
   (cold)
5. In the summer, Los Angeles is almost _____ New York.
   (hot)
6. Los Angeles is _____ New York.
   (wet)
7. Los Angeles is _____ New York.
   (windy)
8. New York is _____ Los Angeles.
   (sunny)

5 CAUSE AND EFFECT WITH TWO COMPARATIVES

Research suggests that there is a connection between the crime rate in U.S. cities and certain other factors. Read the information. Rewrite the information, using two comparatives.

1. When cities are large, they usually have high crime rates.

   The larger the city, the higher the crime rate.

2. When cities are small, they usually have low crime rates.

   _____

3. When cities have warm climates, the police are usually busy.

   _____

4. When the weather is cold, there is usually a great number of robberies.

   _____

5. When the police force is large, the city is usually violent.

   _____

6. When it's late in the day, the number of car thefts is usually high.

   _____

7. When the unemployment rate is high, the crime rate is usually also high.

   _____

8. When the population is mobile (people move from place to place), the city is usually dangerous.

   _____

9. When communities are organized, neighborhoods are usually safe.

   _____

6 THE COMPARATIVE TO EXPRESS CHANGE

Look at these graphs. They show trends in the capital of the United States, Washington, D.C. Make statements about the trends. Use the comparative form of the adjectives in parentheses ( ).

1. Population

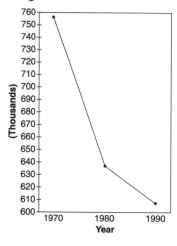

The population of Washington, D.C.,

_____is getting smaller and smaller._____
(small)

2. Population Per Square Mile

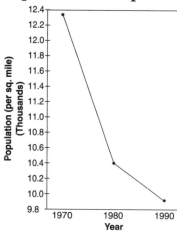

Washington, D.C., _____
(crowded)

3. Unemployment

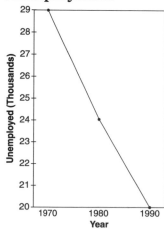

The number of unemployed people

_____
(low)

4. Personal Income

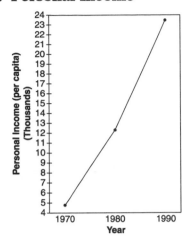

Personal income _____
(high)

5. Average House Price

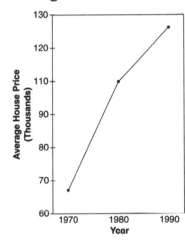

Homes _____
(expensive)

7 **PERSONALIZATION**

Write about trends in your country or city.

1. My city is getting more and more crowded. _____

2. _____

3. _____

4. _____

5. _____

24 ADJECTIVES: SUPERLATIVES

1 SPELLING: REGULAR AND IRREGULAR SUPERLATIVES

Write the superlative form of the adjectives.

Adjective	Superlative
1. nice	the nicest
2. funny	
3. big	
4. wonderful	
5. good	
6. bad	
7. happy	
8. important	
9. warm	
10. interesting	
11. far	
12. intelligent	
13. slow	
14. expensive	

2 THE SUPERLATIVE

*Look at the newspaper ads for three cameras on the next page and complete the conversation between a customer and salesclerk. Use the superlative form (**the . . . -est** or **the most / the least**) of the adjectives in parentheses ( ). Also, write the name of the camera they are talking about.*

Low Price of
$49⁹⁸

RIKON

• Compact 35mm • Built-in Flash with red-eye reduction • Focus-Free • Auto Film Loading • Auto Advance • Auto Exposure

FUNJI
$39⁹⁸

• Focus-Free 35mm with film and batteries • Focus-Free operation • Motorized Auto Advance • Built-in Flash • Drop-in Loading

MINON
$129⁹⁸ $99⁹⁸

•Special One-Time Offer • 35–60mm Zoom Lens • Auto Focus • Built-in Automatic Flash • Ultra Compact— Fits in Your Pocket • Weighs 14 oz.

CLERK: Can I help you?

CUSTOMER: Yes. I'm looking for a camera for my daughter. I want to spend between $40 and $100. What's _____the best_____ camera you have in that
     1. (good)
price range?

CLERK: Well, there are three cameras I can show you. _____
                                                        2. (expensive)
is the _____. It sells for only $39.98.
       3.

CUSTOMER: And how much is _____?
                              4. (expensive)

CLERK: That's the _____. It's on sale for $99.98, and I can
            5.
guarantee that that's _____ price in town. It usually
                       6. (low)
sells for $130.00.

CUSTOMER: How are the three cameras different?

CLERK: Well, the _____ is _____.
                     7.   **8. (small)**
It can fit right inside your pocket.

CUSTOMER: That sounds good. I guess it's _____, too.
                                            9. (light)

CLERK: No, not really. It's the only one of the three with a zoom lens. That makes it
_____ because it brings the picture closer to you.
     10. (powerful)
But it also makes the camera _____. It weighs 14
                              11. (heavy)
ounces. The other two weigh only 10 ounces.

CUSTOMER: I see. What about flashes?

CLERK: All three come with a built-in flash. But the _____
                                                        12.

(continued on next page)

turns on automatically when there isn't enough light. That makes it

_____. Oh, you should also know about a special
        13. (convenient)
feature of the _____. It has what's called "red-eye
                              14.
reduction." That means that when you take a picture of a person and use the

flash, the person's eyes won't look red. That's often a problem when you use a

flash.

CUSTOMER: Oh, that's probably _____ feature in my daughter's
                                        15. (important)
case. She only takes pictures of flowers and trees!

❸ THE SUPERLATIVE

*Complete these world facts. Use the superlative form of the correct
adjectives from the box.*

busy	expensive	fast	~~large~~	popular	small
deep	far	heavy	long	slow	tall

1. Russia is 6,590,876 square miles (17,070,289 square kilometers). It's

   _____the largest_____ country in the world.

2. The Republic of Maldives is only 115 square miles (294 square kilometers). It's

   _____ country in the world.

3. The Pacific Ocean has a depth of 13,215 feet (4,028 meters). It's _____

   ocean in the world.

4. The Petronas Tower in Chicago has 110 floors with a height of 1,482 feet (452 meters).

   It's _____ building in the world.

5. The Seikan Tunnel in Japan stretches for 33.49 miles (53.9 kilometers). It's

   _____ tunnel in the world.

6. The planet Pluto is 3,666 million miles from the sun. It's _____

   planet from the sun.

7. In one year, O'Hare airport in Chicago serves more than 66,000,000 passengers. It's

   _____ airport in the world.

8. France gets more than 61,500,000 visitors a year. It's _____ vacation

destination in the world.

9. The cost of living in Tokyo is very high. In fact, Tokyo is _____ city

in the world.

10. The cheetah (an animal in the cat family) runs 70 mph. It's _____

animal in the world.

11. The garden snail moves at a speed of only 0.03 mph. It's _____

animal in the world.

12. The African elephant weighs 14,432 pounds (7,000 kilograms). It's

_____ land animal in the world.

ADVERBS:
EQUATIVES, COMPARATIVES, SUPERLATIVES

1 SPELLING: REGULAR AND IRREGULAR COMPARATIVE AND SUPERLATIVE FORMS OF ADVERBS

Write the comparative and superlative form of the adverbs.

Adverb	Comparative	Superlative
1. quickly	more quickly	the most quickly
2. fast		
3. beautifully		
4. soon		
5. dangerously		
6. well		
7. early		
8. carefully		
9. badly		
10. far		

2 THE COMPARATIVE FORM OF ADVERBS

*Here is what basketball players from two teams said about the game they played. Complete their comments. Use the correct form of the words in parentheses ( ). Use **than** when necessary.*

GEORGE: The other team played well, but we played much

_____ better _____. That's why we got the results
      1. (good)
we did.

* * * * * *

BOB: We played _____ our opponents. We
                    2. (hard)
deserved to win, and we did.

ALEX: It wasn't a great game for me. I moved _____

3. (slow)

usual because of my bad ankle. In a few weeks I should be able to run

_____. I hope that'll help the team.

4. (fast)

*   *   *   *   *   *

RICK: Our shooting was off today. We missed too many baskets. We need to shoot

_____ if we want to win.

5. (accurate)

*   *   *   *   *   *

LARRY: I was surprised by how well they played. They played

_____ they've played in a long time. We couldn't beat

6. (aggressive)

them.

*   *   *   *   *   *

ELVIN: I'm disappointed. We've been playing a lot _____ our

7. (bad)

opponents this season. We really have to try to concentrate much

_____ in order to break this losing streak.

8. (good)

*   *   *   *   *   *

RANDY: Team spirit was very strong. We played a lot _____

9. (successful)

together, and it paid off.

*   *   *   *   *   *

DENNIS: Of course I'm happy with the results. But if we want to keep it up, we have to

practice _____ and _____

10. (serious)   11. (regular)

we have been. I think we got lucky today.

Now write the names of the players under the correct team.

Winning Team	**Losing Team**
George	_____
_____	_____
_____	_____
_____	_____

❸ COMPARISON OF ADVERBS WITH *AS . . . AS*

Look at these track-and-field records for five athletes. Then complete the statements about them. Use the cues and **(not) as . . . as**.

Event	100 Meter Run	High Jump	Discus Throw
Athlete A	9 min. 36 sec.	7 ft. 9³/₄ in.	217 ft. 2 in.
Athlete B	10 min. 02 sec	6 ft. 8¹/₄ in.	233 ft.
Athlete C	9 min. 59 sec.	7 ft. 10 in.	220 ft. 6 in.
Athlete D	10 min. 02 sec.	7 ft. 10 in.	233 ft.
Athlete E	10 min. 18 sec.	7 ft. 11 in.	233 ft. 1 in.

1. Athlete B _____didn't run as fast as_____ Athlete A.
   (run / fast)

2. Athlete B _____ Athlete D.
   (run / fast)

3. Athlete C _____ Athlete D.
   (jump / high)

4. Athlete A _____ Athlete E.
   (jump / high)

5. Athlete C _____ Athlete E.
   (throw the discus / far)

6. Athlete D _____ Athlete B.
   (throw the discus / far)

7. All in all, Athlete B _____ Athlete D.
   (do / good)

8. All in all, Athlete A _____ Athlete C.
   (compete / successful)

❹ THE COMPARATIVE AND THE SUPERLATIVE OF ADVERBS

Look at the chart in Exercise 3. Complete the statements with the correct form of the words in parentheses ( ). Use **than** *when necessary. Fill in the blanks with the correct athlete—A, B, C, D, or E.*

1. Athlete B ran _____faster than_____ Athlete _E_ , but Athlete _A_ ran
   (fast)
   _____the fastest_____ of all.
   (fast)

2. Athlete ____ ran _____ . He ran _____
   (slow)   (slow)
   all the other players.

3. Athlete A jumped _____ Athlete ____ .
   (high)

4. Athlete ____ jumped _____ of all five athletes.
   (high)

5. Athletes B and D didn't throw the discus _____ Athlete ____.
(far)

6. Athlete ____ threw the discus _____.
(far)

7. Athlete ____ won in two categories. He performed _____.
(good)

---

5 THE COMPARATIVE OF ADVERBS TO EXPRESS CHANGE

Read about these athletes. Then make a statement about each. Use the correct form of the words in the box.

accurate	far	frequent	hard	slow
dangerous	~~fast~~	graceful	high	

1. Last month Lisa ran a mile in twelve minutes. This month she's running a mile in eight minutes.

   She's running faster and faster.

2. Last month she ran three times a week. This month she's running every day.

_____

3. Last month Josh only threw the ball ten yards. This month he's throwing it thirteen yards.

_____

4. Last month when Jennifer shot baskets, she got only five balls in. Now when she shoots baskets, she gets at least eight balls in.

_____

5. Six months ago Mike jumped only four and a half feet. Now he's jumping almost six feet.

_____

6. Matt used to run an eight-minute mile. These days he can only run a ten-minute mile.

_____

7. The ice-skating team of Sonia and Boris used to get four points for artistic impression. These days they are scoring more than five points.

_____

(continued on next page)

8. The members of the basketball team used to practice two hours a day. Now they're practicing three hours a day.

_____

9. Jason drives a race car. Last year he had two accidents. This year he's already had five accidents.

_____

6 EDITING

Read Luisa's exercise journal. Find and correct seven mistakes in the use of adverbs. The first mistake is already corrected.

4/14/01

I just completed my run. I'm running much longer ~~that~~ **than** before. Today I ran for thirty minutes without getting out of breath. I'm glad I decided to run more slow. The more slowly I run, the farthest I can go. I'm really seeing progress. Because I'm enjoying it, I run more and more frequent. And the more often I do it, the longer and farther I can go. I really believe that running helps me feel better more quick than other forms of exercise. I'm even sleeping better than before!

I'm thinking about running in the next marathon. I may not run as fast than younger runners, but I think I can run long and farther. We'll see!

UNIT

26

GERUNDS:
SUBJECT AND OBJECT

1 GERUNDS AS SUBJECT AND AS OBJECT

Complete this article in a health magazine. Use the gerund form of the verbs in parentheses ( ).

KICK UP YOUR HEELS!

In recent years ___dancing___ has become a
1. (dance)
very popular way to stay in shape. In addition to its

health benefits, it also has social advantages. "I enjoy

_____ out and _____
2. (go) **3. (meet)**
new people," says Diana Romero, a 28-year-old word processor.

"_____ all day at a computer isn't healthy. After work I
4. (Sit)
need to move." And Diana isn't alone on the dance floor. Many people

who dislike _____, _____ weights, or
5. (run) **6. (lift)**
_____ sit-ups are swaying to the beat of the swing, salsa,
7. (do)
and rumba. So, if you are looking for an enjoyable way to build muscles

and friendships, consider _____ a spin on one of the
8. (take)
many studio dance floors that are opening up in cities across the

country. "_____ can be fun," says Sandra Carrone, owner
9. (Exercise)
of Studio Two-Step. So, quit _____ time, grab a partner,
10. (waste)
and kick up your heels!

2 GERUNDS AS SUBJECT AND AS OBJECT

*Look at the results of this questionnaire on four people's likes and
dislikes. Then complete the sentences below with appropriate gerunds.*

Key: **+** = enjoy
     ✓ = don't mind
     − = dislike

	Diana	**Hector**	**Minh**	**Amy**
1. dance	+	−	+	−
2. walk	+	+	+	+
3. do sit-ups	−	+	−	−
4. play tennis	−	✓	+	−
5. jog	−	+	✓	−
6. lift weights	✓	✓	−	+

1. Hector is the only one who enjoys _____ *doing sit-ups* _____.

2. Minh doesn't like _____, but Diana doesn't mind it.

3. Minh really enjoys _____, but Diana and Amy both dislike

   it.

4. Diana enjoys _____, but Amy really dislikes it.

5. _____ is the activity that people most disliked.

6. Half of the people don't mind _____.

7. _____ is an activity that half of the people enjoy.

8. _____ is the only activity that all four enjoy.

9. Diana and Minh are going to go _____ together at the Two-

   Step Studio. They both enjoy it.

10. Minh doesn't mind _____.

11. Amy and Diana dislike _____.

12. They also dislike _____.

3 GERUNDS AFTER CERTAIN VERBS

Sandra Carrone is having a dance party at her studio. Complete the summary sentences with the appropriate verbs from the box and use the gerund form of the verbs in parentheses ( ).

admit	deny	enjoy	mind	regret
consider	dislike	keep	~~quit~~	suggest

1.   **MINH:** Would you like a cup of coffee?

  DIANA: No, thanks. I haven't had coffee in five years.

  Diana _____quit drinking_____ coffee five years ago.
  <u>(drink)</u>

2. **OSCAR:** Oh, they're playing a tango. Would you like to dance?

  RIKA: No, thanks. It's not my favorite dance.

  Rika _____ the tango.
  <u>(do)</u>

3.   **AMY:** Do you often come to these dance parties?

  MARIA: Yes. It's a good opportunity to dance with a lot of different partners.

  Maria _____ with different partners.
  <u>(dance)</u>

4. **LAURA:** I don't know how to do the cha-cha. Could you show me?

  BILL: OK. Just follow me.

  Bill doesn't _____ Laura the cha-cha.
  <u>(teach)</u>

5. **DIANA:** This is a difficult dance. How did you learn it?

  MINH: I practiced it again and again.

  Minh _____ the dance.
  <u>(practice)</u>

6. **VERA:** Ow. You stepped on my toe!

  LUIS: No, I didn't!

  Luis _____ on Vera's toe.
  <u>(step)</u>

7.   **BILL:** Are you going to take any more classes?

  LAURA: I'm not sure. I haven't decided yet. Maybe.

  Laura is _____ more dance classes.
  <u>(take)</u>

(continued on next page)

8. **DIANA:** I really love dancing.

   MINH: Me too. I'm sorry I didn't start years ago. It's a lot of fun.

   Minh _____ dance lessons sooner.
            (not begin)

9. **BILL:** Why don't we go out for coffee after class next week?

   LAURA: OK. I'd like that.

   Bill _____ out after class.
            (go)

10. **MINH:** You look tired.

   LAURA: I *am* tired. I think this will be the last dance for me.

   Laura _____ tired.
            (feel)

4 PERSONALIZATION

Look at the chart in Exercise 2. How do you feel about the six activities in the chart? Write sentences using **enjoy**, **don't mind**, *or* **dislike**. *If you have never done an activity, begin your sentence with:* **I (don't) think I would enjoy. . . .**

1. _____

2. _____

3. _____

4. _____

5. _____

6. _____

GERUNDS AFTER PREPOSITIONS

1 PREPOSITIONS AFTER CERTAIN VERBS AND ADJECTIVES

Complete the chart with the correct preposition. You will use some prepositions more than once.

about	for	in	of	on	to

1. look forward _____*to*_____

2. be tired _____

3. be used _____

4. insist _____

5. believe _____

6. apologize _____

7. approve _____

8. succeed _____

9. be worried _____

10. be opposed _____

2 GERUNDS AFTER PREPOSITIONS

Read these conversations that take place at a student council meeting. Complete the summary sentences. Use the expressions in Exercise 1 and the gerund form of the verbs in parentheses ( ).

1. **KYLE:** Where were you? It's 7:30. Our meeting started at 7:00.

   JOHN: I know. I'm sorry.

   John _____*apologized for coming*_____ late.
          (come)

(continued on next page)

2. **MATT:** I have some good news. We've reached our goal. Since our last meeting, we've

collected more than 100 student signatures in favor of going on strike.

The students _____ more than 100 signatures.
(collect)

3. **AMY:** I'm not so sure it's a good idea to strike.

JOHN: Final exams are in a few weeks. It'll be a problem if we miss classes.

John _____ classes.
(miss)

4. **AMY:** I don't know. We've always solved our problems with the administration before.

JOHN: That's true. In the past they've always listened to us.

These students _____ together with the administration.
(work)

5. **AMY:** I'm against striking. We should talk to the administration again.

JOHN: I agree. That's the best way to solve this problem.

Amy and John _____ to the administration again.
(talk)

6. **MATT:** We keep asking the administration for a response. They've said nothing.

EVA: That's right. We've had enough. We don't want to wait any more.

These students _____ for an answer.
(wait)

7. **JOHN:** Can we give this decision a little more time?

MATT: No, I'm sorry. We really *have to* reach a decision today.

Matt _____ a decision immediately.
(reach)

8. **MATT:** Let's take a vote. All those in favor of going on strike raise your hand. . . . OK.

That's 10 for and 2 against. We'll recommend a strike to the student body.

The student council _____ a strike.
(have)

9. **EVA:** Only two people voted no.

Only two council members _____ on strike.
(go)

10. **AMY:** I don't know about you, but I'll be glad when all this is over.

JOHN: I know what you mean. I'll be happy when things return to normal.

Amy and John are _____ to their normal activities.
(return)

3 GERUNDS AFTER PREPOSITIONS

Complete this editorial in the student newspaper. Use the gerund form of the appropriate verbs from the box.

be	get	hear	miss	strike
fire	~~go~~	make	permit	try

Yesterday the student council voted 10 to 2 in favor of _____going_____ on strike. By
1.
_____, they hope to reverse the
2.
administration's decision to fire two popular

teachers. The students are very much against

_____ teachers because of their
3.
political views. They strongly believe in

_____ the free expression of all
4.
opinions. They feel that teachers, as well as

students, should be able to say what they want

without _____ afraid of the
5.
administration's reaction.

If the student council succeeds in

_____ student support, the
6.

strike will begin on Tuesday. Not all students,

however, support the idea of a strike. Many are

afraid of _____ classes just a
7.
few weeks before exam time. They haven't

given up _____ to solve the
8.
problem with the administration. Other

students haven't made up their minds yet.

Which side are you on? Before

_____ a final decision, we
9.
suggest that you attend the students' meeting

on Monday at 4:00. After _____
10.
both sides, it may be easier to make a decision.

4 PERSONALIZATION

How do you feel about school? Complete these sentences by adding a preposition and a gerund.

1. I'm looking forward _____

2. I'm a little worried _____

3. I've gotten used _____

4. I sometimes get tired _____

INFINITIVES AFTER CERTAIN VERBS

 INFINITIVES AFTER CERTAIN VERBS

Read this exchange of letters in an advice column. Use the cues to complete the letters. Choose the correct tense of the first verb and use the infinitive form of the second verb.

Dear Gabby,

I've known John for two years. Last month after a lot of discussion, we

_____decided to get_____ married. Since then our relationship has
　　　　　1. (decide / get)
been a nightmare. John criticizes me for every little thing, and we are constantly

fighting. I _____ a marriage counselor, but John
　　　　　　　　2. (want / see)
_____ with me. Last night he even
　　　3. (refuse / go)
_____ the relationship if I mention the idea of
　　4. (threaten / end)
counseling again.

I don't understand what's going on. We used to get along great. I still love

John, but I _____ the next step.
　　　　　　　5. (hesitate / take)
What should I do?

One Step Out the Door

> *Dear One Step Out the Door,*
>
> I've heard your story many times before. You're right to be concerned. John
>
> _____ afraid of getting married. As soon as
> **6. (seem / be)**
> you got engaged, he _____ distance by fighting
> **7. (attempt / create)**
> with you. I agree that counseling is a good idea if the two of you really
>
> _____ together. Maybe each of you
> **8. (intend / stay)**
> _____ to a counselor separately before going to
> **9. (need / speak)**
> one together. It's possible that John _____ alone
> **10. (agree / go)**
> to discuss some of his fears.
>
> *Gabby*

② VERB + INFINITIVE OR VERB + OBJECT + INFINITIVE

Read some conversations that take place between men and women in relationships. Complete the summary statements.

1. **SHE:** I *really* think you should see a therapist.

   HE: I'm not going to.

   She urged _him to see a therapist._____

   He refused _to see a therapist._____

2. **HE:** You do the dishes.

   SHE: No, you do the dishes.

   He didn't want _____

   She wanted _____

3. **HE:** Don't forget to buy some milk.

   SHE: OK. I'll get some on the way home.

   He reminded _____

   She agreed _____

(continued on next page)

4. SHE: Will you do me a favor? Could you drive me to my aunt's?

   HE: OK.

   She asked _____

   He agreed _____

5. SHE: Would you like to have dinner at my place Friday night?

   HE: Uhm. I'm not sure. Uhm. I guess so.

   She invited _____

   He hesitated _____

6. SHE: Will you give me your answer tomorrow?

   HE: Yes, I will. That's a promise.

   She wants _____

   He promised _____

7. SHE: Would you like me to cut your hair? It's really long.

   HE: Oh, OK.

   She offered _____

   He is going to allow _____

8. SHE: It's 8:00. I thought you said you'd be home at 7:00.

   HE: No. I always get home at 8:00.

   She expected _____

   He expected _____

9. HE: Could you call me before you leave the office?

   SHE: I was going to, but I forgot.

   He would like _____

   She intended _____

3 EDITING

Read this journal entry. Find and correct six mistakes in the use of infinitives. The first mistake is already corrected.

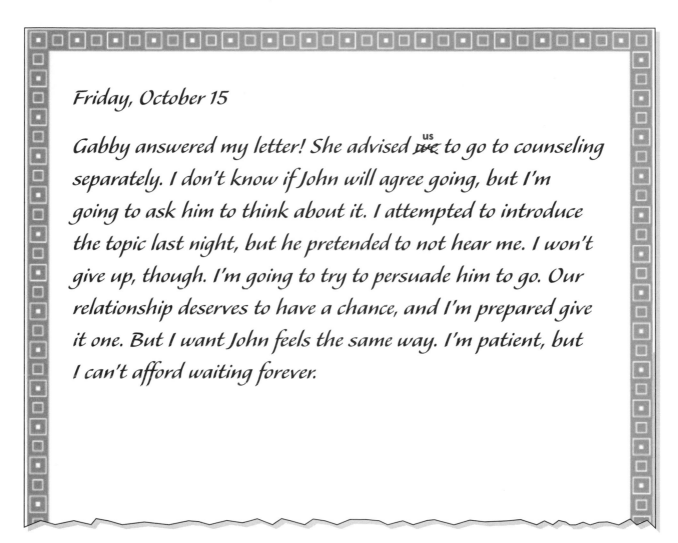

> Friday, October 15
>
> Gabby answered my letter! She advised ~~me~~ ^{us} to go to counseling separately. I don't know if John will agree going, but I'm going to ask him to think about it. I attempted to introduce the topic last night, but he pretended to not hear me. I won't give up, though. I'm going to try to persuade him to go. Our relationship deserves to have a chance, and I'm prepared give it one. But I want John feels the same way. I'm patient, but I can't afford waiting forever.

4 PERSONALIZATION

What do you expect from your friends? Write about yourself. Use infinitives.

1. I expect _____

2. I would like _____

3. I urge _____

4. I try to persuade _____

5. _____

INFINITIVES OF PURPOSE

1 AFFIRMATIVE AND NEGATIVE STATEMENTS

Read the pairs of sentences. Combine them, using the infinitive of purpose.

1. I went to Lacy's department store. I wanted to buy some clothes.

   I went to Lacy's department store to buy some clothes.

2. He bought an alarm clock. He didn't want to oversleep.

   He bought an alarm clock in order not to oversleep.

3. She used her credit card. She didn't want to pay right away.

   _____

4. I asked for the dressing room. I wanted to try on a dress.

   _____

5. They went to the snack bar. They wanted to get a drink.

   _____

6. I'm going to wait for a sale. I want to save some money.

   _____

7. She tried on the blouse. She wanted to be sure of the size.

   _____

8. He only took fifty dollars with him. He didn't want to spend more.

   _____

9. They went to Lacy's on Monday. They didn't want to miss the sale.

   _____

10. I always go shopping early. I want to avoid the crowds.

    _____

2 AFFIRMATIVE AND NEGATIVE STATEMENTS

These conversations take place in a department store. Complete them.
Use the verbs in the box and the infinitive of purpose.

~~ask~~	cut	have	pay	sign
carry	find out	miss	return	waste

1. **A:** Before we start looking around, I want to go to the information desk.

   B: Oh. Why do you need to go there?

   A: _____ *To ask* _____ where the petites department is. I can never find

   it. They keep changing its location.

2. **A:** I'd like to return this.

   B: Do you have the receipt?

   A: No, I don't. I got it as a gift, and I really can't use it.

   B: Hmm. I see there's no price tag on it. I'm sorry, but you need the receipt or the

   price tag _____ it.

3. **A:** Do you always pay by credit card?

   B: Most of the time. What about you?

   A: No. I don't like to pay finance charges. It ends up being more expensive that way.

   B: I know what you mean. I always pay the bill immediately _____

   a finance charge.

4. **A:** Can I please have a shopping bag?

   B: Sure.

   A: Thanks. I need one _____ all this stuff.

5. **A:** Do you have a pen?

   B: Here you are.

   A: Thanks. I need one _____ my name.

(continued on next page)

6. **A:** I'm hungry.

   B: Me too. Let's go to the food court _____ a snack.

   A: Good idea. I always get hungry when I go shopping.

7. **A:** Do you have a sharper knife? I need one _____ this

   steak. It's a little tough.

   B: I'm sorry. I'll bring you one right away.

8. **A:** How do those shoes fit?

   B: I'm not sure. They may be a little tight.

   A: Walk around a little _____ if they're the right size.

9. **A:** We should leave now.

   B: Why? It's only 5:00.

   A: I know. But we have to leave now _____ the express bus.

10. **A:** Here's the up escalator, but where's the escalator going down?

    B: Oh, let's just take the elevator _____ time.

❸ EDITING

Read this note. Find and correct four mistakes in the use of the infinitive of purpose. The first mistake is already corrected.

> Eva—
>
>   I went to the store ~~for~~ to get some eggs and other things for dinner.
> I set the alarm on the electronic organizer to remind you to put the
> turkey in the oven. Could you call Cindi too ask her to bring some
> dessert? Tell her she should come straight from school in order to be
> not late. We'll eat at 6:00—if that's OK with you. Remember—you
> can use the Datalator for checking the vegetable casserole recipe. I've
> got to run in order to get back in time to help you!
>
>   M.

INFINITIVES
WITH *TOO* AND *ENOUGH*

1 WORD ORDER

Put the words in the correct order to make sentences about a new job.

1. near / for me / it's / to walk to work / enough

  It's near enough for me to walk to work.   **+**

2. too / it's / noisy / for me / to concentrate

_____

3. varied / to be interesting / the work / enough / is

_____

4. for me / the salary / enough / to support my family / is / high

_____

5. to hold / my desk / small / is / too / all my things

_____

6. late / I / sleep / enough / can / to feel awake in the morning

_____

7. for me / my boss / quickly / to understand him / speaks / too

_____

8. aren't / low / the bookshelves / to reach / for me / enough

_____

Now look at the sentences you wrote. Put a plus (+) next to all the positive points. Put a minus (–) next to all the negative points.

2 INFINITIVES WITH *TOO* AND *ENOUGH*

Complete these conversations that take place at the workplace.

1. **A:** Can you read the boss's handwriting?

   B: No. It's _____ too messy for me to read _____.

              (messy / me / read)

2. **A:** It's 11:00 A.M. Do you think we can call Mr. Lin in San Francisco?

   B: Sure. It's 8:00 A.M. there. That's _____.

              (late / call)

3. **A:** Could you help me with those boxes?

   B: Sorry. They're _____. I have a bad back.

              (heavy / me / carry)

4. **A:** You're not drinking your coffee! What's the matter with it?

   B: It's _____. It tastes like someone put about four

              (sweet / drink)

   tablespoons of sugar in it.

5. **A:** Do you think we can put the fax machine on that shelf?

   B: Sure. It's _____.

              (small / fit)

6. **A:** Can you keep the noise down, please? It's _____.

              (noisy / me / think)

   B: Sorry. We'll try to be quieter.

7. **A:** Did you hear that Alex is retiring?

   B: You're kidding! He's not even fifty. He's _____.

              (old / retire)

8. **A:** Can you turn on the air conditioner, please?

   B: The air conditioner! It's _____ the air conditioner.

              (hot / need)

   What are you going to do in August when it really gets hot?

9. **A:** You sound really sick. Maybe you should call the doctor.

   B: Oh. I'm _____ the doctor. I just need to get some rest.

              (sick / call)

10. **A:** Can you help me get that box? It's _____.

               (high / me / reach)

    B: Sure.

❸ EDITING

Read this letter home from a boy in Boy Scout camp. Find and correct seven mistakes in the use of the infinitive with **too** *and* **enough**. *The first mistake is already corrected.*

Dear Mom and Dad,

    I'm almost ~~to~~ **too** tired to write. I can't believe how hard Boy Scout camp is.

○ Today we went out on a two-hour hike. It was over 90° in the shade! It was

too hot for to think. We had to take a lot of stuff with us, too. My backpack

was too heavy for me to lift it. I don't think I'm too strong to complete the

program. How did I get into this mess? Is it too late too get out?

Please write.

Love,

Andy

○ P.S. The food is terrible. It's not enough good to eat. Can

you send some candy bars?

P.P.S. Here's a photo of me in case it's been to long for

you to remember what I look like!

---

❹ PERSONALIZATION

Complete these sentences about your home or classroom.

1. It's too _____

2. It's _____ enough _____

3. It isn't too _____

4. It isn't _____ enough _____

GERUNDS AND INFINITIVES

Complete this notice about neighborhood crime prevention. Use the correct form of the verbs in parentheses ( ).

Join Your Neighborhood Watch

_____Making_____ our neighborhood safe is our main concern.
    1. (make)
Here are some safety tips:

• Remember _____to lock_____ your doors and windows when you go out.
    2. (lock)

• Don't forget _____ some lights on when you're not at home.
    3. (leave)

• Avoid _____ alone on dark, deserted streets.
    4. (walk)

• Learn _____ aware of your surroundings.
    5. (be)

• Don't stop _____ for your house keys. Have them in your hand
    6. (look)
before you get to the door.

• Consider _____ a class in self-defense. The Adult Center offers
    7. (take)
free classes.

• Don't hesitate _____ a police officer for help.
    8. (ask)
It's better to be safe than sorry. Stop _____ in
    9. (live)
fear. Join your Neighborhood Watch.

The next meeting is at 7:00 P.M. Tuesday, March 3, at the

Community Center.

Please attend! We look forward to _____ you there!
    10. (see)

---

2 GERUND OR INFINITIVE

These conversations took place at a community center. Complete the summary statements about them. Choose the right verbs or expressions from the box and use the gerund or infinitive form of the verbs in parentheses ( ).

afford	be tired of	~~enjoy~~	intend	quit	remember
agree	believe in	forget	offer	refuse	stop

1.   **JOE:** Have you ever been to one of these meetings before?

   NANCY: Yes. You get a lot of useful tips. Besides, I like to meet my neighbors.

   Nancy _____*enjoys meeting*_____ her neighbors.
                       (meet)

2.   **ANDREA:** Why did you start coming to these meetings?

   FRANK: My apartment was broken into twice. I've had enough. I want to do

   something about it.

   Frank _____ a crime victim.
                 (be)

3.   **CRAIG:** Would you like a cup of coffee?

   SYLVIE: Oh, no thanks.

   CRAIG: Don't you drink coffee?

   SYLVIE: I used to, but I gave it up a year ago.

   Sylvie _____ coffee.
               (drink)

4.   **CARYN:** I think these meetings are really important. You can get a lot accomplished

   when you work with other people.

   FERNANDO: I know what you mean.

   Caryn _____ with other people.
               (work)

5.   **JANE:** Did you bring Gerry's book?

   SARA: Oh, no. I left it at work.

   Jane _____ Gerry's book.
              (bring)

6.   **SHARON:** Did you lock the windows before we left the house?

   JIM: No, *you* locked the windows. I saw you do it.

   SHARON: That's strange. I don't _____ them!
                                            (lock)

(continued on next page)

7. **TOM:** You're late. I was getting worried.

    BETSY: I'm sorry. On the way over here, I noticed that I was almost out of gas. So I

    went to fill up the tank.

    Betsy _____ gas.

(get)

8. **CATHY:** I really don't like the neighborhood anymore.

    MIKE: So why don't you move?

    CATHY: The rents are too high everywhere else.

    Cathy can't _____.

(move)

9. **CAMILLE:** I was afraid to come to the meeting tonight.

    VILMA: Well, I just *won't* live in fear.

    Vilma _____ in fear.

(live)

10. **SARA:** Do you have a burglar alarm?

    DAVE: No. But I'm definitely going to get one.

    Dave _____ a burglar alarm.

(get)

11. **RACHEL:** Do you think you could help us organize the next meeting?

    WALTER: OK. When is it scheduled for?

    RACHEL: We don't have a date yet, but I'll let you know.

    Walter _____ with the next meeting.

(help)

12. **AXEL:** Would you like a ride home?

    JOANNA: Thanks. That would be great.

    AXEL: We'll be leaving in about five minutes.

    JOANNA: I'll be ready.

    Axel _____ Joanna home.

(drive)

3 GERUND OR INFINITIVE

Rewrite these sentences. Use the gerund or infinitive.

1. It's important to know your neighbors.

   Knowing your neighbors is important.

2. Going to the community center is fun.

   It's fun to go to the community center.

3. It's wise to be cautious.

   _____

4. Walking on ice is dangerous.

   _____

5. Installing a burglar alarm is a good idea.

   _____

6. It's not good to be afraid all the time.

   _____

7. Walking alone on a dark, deserted street is risky.

   _____

8. Working together is helpful.

   _____

4 PERSONALIZATION

Write about safety measures you take. Use gerunds and infinitives.

1. I avoid _____

2. I always try _____

3. It's important _____

4. I keep _____

5. I try to remember _____

6. _____

UNIT

PREFERENCES:
PREFER, WOULD PREFER, WOULD RATHER

❶ AFFIRMATIVE STATEMENTS

Alicia ranked the following leisure-time activities according to her preferences. (1 = what Alicia likes most; 10 = what Alicia likes least.)

> **Leisure-Time Preferences**
>
> _5_ cook
> _3_ watch TV
> _2_ go to the movies
> _1_ read a book
> _10_ play cards
> _9_ go for a walk
> _4_ visit friends
> _7_ talk on the phone
> _6_ eat out
> _8_ listen to music

Write about Alicia's preferences.

1. cook / eat out

   Alicia prefers _____ cooking to eating out. _____

2. listen to music / go for a walk

   She'd rather _____

3. read a book / visit friends

   She prefers _____

4. visit friends / talk on the phone

   She prefers _____

5. watch TV / go to the movies

   She'd rather _____

6. talk on the phone / listen to music

She'd rather _____

7. play cards / go to the movies

She prefers _____

8. watch TV / listen to music

She prefers _____

9. read a book / watch TV

She'd rather _____

10. play cards / read a book

She prefers _____

❷ AFFIRMATIVE AND NEGATIVE STATEMENTS

Ralph is in the hospital. He completed this meal form.

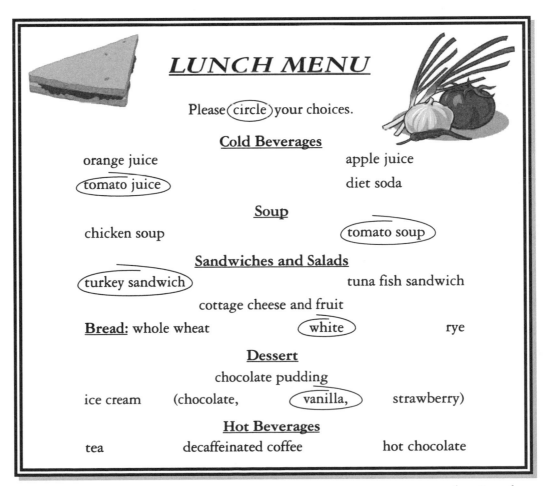

LUNCH MENU

Please (circle) your choices.

Cold Beverages

orange juice   apple juice

(tomato juice)   diet soda

Soup

chicken soup   (tomato soup)

Sandwiches and Salads

(turkey sandwich)   tuna fish sandwich

cottage cheese and fruit

Bread: whole wheat   (white)   rye

Dessert

chocolate pudding

ice cream   (chocolate,   (vanilla,)   strawberry)

Hot Beverages

tea   decaffeinated coffee   hot chocolate

(continued on next page)

Use the cues to make sentences about Ralph's preferences.

1. He'd rather / diet soda

   He'd rather not have diet soda.

2. He'd prefer / juice

   _____

3. He'd rather / apple juice / tomato juice

   _____

4. He'd rather / a hot beverage

   _____

5. He'd prefer / chicken soup

   _____

6. He'd prefer / a sandwich / cottage cheese and fruit

   _____

7. He'd prefer / a tuna fish sandwich / a turkey sandwich

   _____

8. He'd rather / white bread

   _____

9. Hc'd rather / chocolate pudding

   _____

10. He'd prefer / chocolate ice cream / vanilla ice cream

   _____

③ QUESTIONS

Complete these conversations with **do you prefer**, **would you prefer**, *or* **would you rather**.

1. **A:** _____ Do you prefer _____ watching TV or going to the movies?

   B: It really depends. If there's something good on TV, I like doing that.

2. **A:** _____ newspapers to magazines?

   B: Oh. I definitely prefer newspapers.

3. **A:** I don't feel like going out.

   B: _____ stay home?

   A: Yes, I think I would.

4. **A:** I've got vanilla and chocolate ice cream. Which _____ have?

   B: Chocolate, please.

5. **A:** I thought we could stay home tonight.

   B: Really?

   A: _____ go out?

   B: Well, there's a good movie at the Quad.

6. **A:** There's a show at 8:00 and one at 10:00. _____ the early or the late show?

   B: Let's go to the early show.

7. **A:** Could you get me some juice?

   B: Sure. _____ orange or grapefruit?

   A: Orange, please.

8. **A:** How do you like to spend your free time? _____ doing things with friends or doing things alone?

   B: It depends. I need time for my friends, and I need time to be alone.

④ PERSONALIZATION

Look at the menu in Exercise 2. Complete these sentences with true information.

1. I'd prefer _____

2. I'd rather not _____

3. I'd prefer not _____

 NECESSITY: HAVE (GOT) TO, DON'T HAVE TO, MUST, MUST NOT, CAN'T

1 AFFIRMATIVE AND NEGATIVE STATEMENTS WITH *MUST*

*Complete these rules from the California driver's handbook. Use the words in the box with **must** or **must not**.*

allow	drink	~~have~~	send	turn on
be	drive	place	stop	wear

1. If you are a resident of California and drive a motor vehicle on a public highway, you _____must have_____ a California driver's license.

2. You _____ your child under the age of 18 years to drive on a highway without a license or permit.

3. An instruction permit does not allow you to drive alone. An adult who has a driver's license _____ in the car with you.

4. When you move, you _____ your new address to the Department of Motor Vehicles in ten days.

5. You _____ so slowly that you are a danger on the road. You can get a ticket for driving too slowly as well as for driving too fast.

6. The law says adults _____ their children in approved safety seats (if a child is under 4 years old or weighs less than 40 pounds).

7. The law says you _____ your headlights when you drive from 30

   minutes after sunset until 30 minutes before sunrise, and any other time when you

   can see less than 1,000 feet ahead of you.

8. The driver of a vehicle _____ a headset over, or earplugs in, both

   ears.

9. It is illegal to leave the scene of an accident. You _____ your car.

10. As in all states, driving under the influence of alcohol is against the law in California.

   You _____ and drive!

2   AFFIRMATIVE AND NEGATIVE STATEMENTS WITH *HAVE TO*

In the United States, motor vehicle rules differ from state to state. Look
at the chart. Complete the statements with **have to** *or* **don't have to**
and the verbs in parentheses ( ).

	AGE FOR REGULAR LICENSE	DRIVER'S EDUCATION CLASS REQUIRED	LICENSE DURATION	FEE	ANNUAL SAFETY INSPECTION	SEAT BELT LAW
Alaska	16	No	5 yrs.	$15.00	No	Yes
California	18	No	4 yrs.	$12.00	No	Yes
Florida	16	No	4 yrs.	$20.00	No	Yes
Massachusetts	18	Yes	5 yrs.	$33.75	Yes	Yes
New Hampshire	18	No	4 yrs.	$32.50	Yes	No
New York	17	Yes	4 yrs.	$22.25	Yes	Yes
Texas	16	No	4 yrs.	$16.00	Yes	Yes
Washington, D.C.	16	No	4 yrs.	$10.50	Yes	Yes

(continued on next page)

1. You _____ have to be _____ 18 to get a California driver's license.
   (be)

2. You _____ 18 to get a license in Alaska.
   (be)

3. You _____ a driver's education class in order to get your
   (take)
   license in Florida.

4. You _____ a driver's education course in New York.
   (complete)

5. In Massachusetts, you _____ your license every four years.
   (renew)

6. In Washington, D.C., you _____ your license every four
   (renew)
   years.

7. You _____ a $33.75 fee for a Massachusetts license.
   (pay)

8. You _____ as much for an Alaska license.
   (pay)

9. You _____ your car for a yearly inspection in New York.
   (take)

10. You _____ a yearly inspection in Florida.
    (get)

11. You _____ a seat belt in Texas.
    (wear)

12. You _____ a seat belt in New Hampshire.
    (wear)

❸ CONTRAST: *MUST NOT* OR *DON'T HAVE TO*

Look again at the chart in Exercise 2. Complete these statements with
must not *or* **don't have to**.

1. If you are under the age of 16, you _____ must not _____ drive in the state
   of California.

2. You _____ be 18 to drive in the state of Texas.

3. You _____ take a driver's education course in most of the
   states.

4. You _____ renew your license every four years in
   Massachusetts.

5. You _____ drive with an expired license.

6. You _____ pay a $20.00 license fee in Washington, D.C.

7. You _____ have an annual car inspection in Florida.

8. You _____ forget to have your car inspected annually if you live in Washington, D.C.

9. You _____ drive without a seat belt in Florida.

10. You _____ wear a seat belt in New Hampshire.

---

4 STATEMENTS, QUESTIONS, AND SHORT ANSWERS WITH *HAVE TO*

Complete these conversations. Use the correct form of **have to** *and the verbs in parentheses ( ). Use short answers when necessary. Be sure to use the correct tense.*

1. A: Did you pass your road test the first time you took it?

    B: No. I _____ had to take _____ it two more times before I passed!
                  (take)

2. A: _____ we _____ for gas?
                             (stop)

    B: _____. The tank's almost empty.

3. A: How many times _____ you _____ public
                                    (use)

    transportation since you moved to Los Angeles?

    B: Only once. When my car broke down.

4. A: _____ you _____ late yesterday?
                           (work)

    B: _____. Luckily, I finished on time.

5. A: Are you thinking of buying a new car?

    B: Not yet. But in a couple of years I _____ another one.
                                   (get)

6. A: Why didn't you come to the meeting last night?

    B: I _____ my uncle to the airport.
           (drive)

7. A: My wife got a speeding ticket last week.

    B: Really? How much _____ she

    _____?
       (pay)

    A: It was more than $100.

(continued on next page)

8. **A:** _____ your son ever _____
   (pay)

   for a traffic violation?

   B: _____. He's a very careful driver.

9. **A:** _____ you _____ a new
   (get)

   license when you move?

   B: _____. You can only use an out-of-state license for ten

   days.

10. **A:** Do you have car insurance?

    B: Of course. Everyone in New York _____ car insurance.
    (have)

---

5 **CONTRAST: *MUST, MUST NOT, HAVE TO, DON'T HAVE TO,
AND CAN'T***

*Read these test questions about road signs. Write the letter of the correct
answer in the box.*

---

1. When you see [YIELD] it means:

   a. You must come to a complete stop.
   b. You must not stop.
   c. You don't have to stop, but you must slow down and prepare
   to stop if necessary.

   ANS
   C

2. When you see [STOP] it means:

   a. You don't have to stop.
   b. You must stop.
   c. You can't stop.

   ANS

3. When you see [SPEED LIMIT 50] it means:

   a. You must drive 50 miles per hour.
   b. You must not drive faster than 50 miles per hour.
   c. You don't have to drive more than 50 miles per hour.

   ANS

4. When you see | NO TURN ON RED | it means:

   a. You have to turn when the light is red.
   b. You don't have to turn when the light is red.
   c. You must not turn when the light is red.

ANS ☐

5. When you see | DO NOT ENTER | it means:

   a. You must not enter.
   b. You don't have to enter.
   c. You must enter.

ANS ☐

6. When you see | DO NOT PASS | it means:

   a. You don't have to pass another car.
   b. You can't pass another car.
   c. You have to pass another car.

ANS ☐

7. When you see | ONE WAY > | it means:

   a. You must drive in the direction of the arrow.
   b. You must not drive in the direction of the arrow.
   c. You don't have to drive in the direction of the arrow.

ANS ☐

8. When you see | MAXIMUM SPEED 65 / MINIMUM SPEED 45 | it means:

   a. You have to drive 45 miles per hour or slower.
   b. You can't drive 70 miles per hour.
   c. You don't have to drive 70 miles per hour.

ANS ☐

---

6 PERSONALIZATION

Complete these sentences with information about yourself.

1. Next week, I have to _____

2. I don't have to _____

3. I must not _____

4. I can't _____

EXPECTATIONS:
BE SUPPOSED TO

---

1 **AFFIRMATIVE AND NEGATIVE STATEMENTS WITH *BE SUPPOSED TO***

Today when people get married, the groom's family often shares the expenses, and older couples often pay for their own weddings. However, some people are still traditional. Read the chart and complete the sentences.

Traditional Division of Wedding Expenses	
Responsibilities of the Bride's Family	**Responsibilities of the Groom's Family**
send invitations pay for food supply flowers pay for the groom's ring provide music	pay for the bride's ring give a rehearsal dinner finance the honeymoon

1. The groom's parents <u>aren't supposed to send</u> the invitations.

2. The bride's family _____ the invitations.

3. The bride's parents _____ music.

4. The groom's family _____ the groom's ring.

5. The groom's family _____ the bride's ring.

6. The bride's parents _____ the honeymoon.

7. The groom's family _____ the honeymoon.

8. The bride's parents _____ the rehearsal

   dinner.

9. The groom's family _____ the flowers.

10. The bride's family _____ the food.

2 AFFIRMATIVE AND NEGATIVE STATEMENTS WITH *BE SUPPOSED TO*

Linda Nelson is getting married. She completed this change of address form, but she made eight mistakes. Find the mistakes and write sentences with **was supposed to** *and* **wasn't supposed to**. *Include the number of the item.*

U.S. Postal Service CHANGE OF ADDRESS ORDER	Customer Instructions: Complete Items 1 thru 9, Except Item 8, please PRINT all information including address on face of card.	OFFICIAL USE ONLY
1. Change of address for *(Check one)* ☑ Individual ☑ Entire Family ☐ Business		Zone/Route Id No.
2. Start Date Month Day Year 3 0 0 6 9 5	3. If TEMPORARY address, print date to discontinue forwarding Month Day Year	Date Entered on Form 3982 M M D D Y Y
4. Print Last Name or Name of Business *(If more than one use, use separate Change of Address Order Form for each)* L I N D A		Expiration Date M M D D Y Y
5. Print First Name of Head of Household (include Jr., Sr., etc.). Leave Blank if the Change of Address Order is for a business. N e l s o n		Clerk/Carrier Endorsements
6. Print OLD mailing address, number and street *(if Puerto Rico, include urbanization zone)* 2 6 MAPLE ROAD		
Apt./Suite No. 4 A P.O. Box No. R.R/HCR No. Rural Box/HCR Box No.		
City BOSTON State M A Zip Code –		
7. Print NEW Mailing address, number and street *(if Puerto Rico, include urbanization zone)* 2 9 8 7 COSBY AVE		
Apt./Suite No. P.O. Box No. R.R/HCR No. Rural Box/HCR Box No.		
City AMHERST State Zip Code 0 1 0 0 2 –		
8. Signature *(See conditions on reverse)* Linda Nelson 9. Date Signed Month Day Year	OFFICIAL USE ONLY	
OFFICIAL USE ONLY Verification Endorsement		
PS Form 3575, June 1991		☆ U.S.G.P.O. 1992-309-315

1. Item __1__ _____ She was supposed to check one box. _____

OR

_____ She wasn't supposed to check two boxes. _____

2. Item _____ _____

3. Item _____ _____

4. Item _____ _____

5. Item _____ _____

6. Item _____ _____

7. Item _____ _____

8. Item _____ _____

3 **QUESTIONS AND ANSWERS WITH *BE SUPPOSED TO***

Linda and her new husband are on their honeymoon. Complete the conversations. Use the words in the box and **be supposed to***. Use short answers when necessary.*

~~arrive~~	call	get	leave	shake
be	do	land	rain	tip

1. **LINDA:** What time _____are_____ we _____supposed to arrive_____ in Bermuda?

   FRANK: Well, the plane _____ at 10:30, but it looks like we're

   going to be late.

2. **LINDA:** What time _____ we _____ to the hotel?

   FRANK: Check-in time is 12:00.

3. **LINDA:** _____ we _____ if we're going to be late?

   FRANK: _____. We'd better look for a phone as soon as we

   land.

4. **FRANK:** How much _____ we _____ the person

   who carries our bags?

   LINDA: I think it's $1.00 a bag.

5. **FRANK:** _____ the hotel restaurant _____ good?

   LINDA: _____. The travel agent suggested that we go

   somewhere else for dinner.

6. **LINDA:** What _____ we _____ with our keys when

   we leave the hotel?

   FRANK: We _____ them at the front desk.

7. **LINDA:** _____ it _____ today?

   FRANK: _____. But look at those clouds. I think we'd better

   take an umbrella just in case.

8. **LINDA:** Can you hand me that bottle of sunblock?

   FRANK: Sure. _____ you _____ the bottle before

   you use it?

   LINDA: I don't know. What do the instructions say?

FUTURE POSSIBILITY: MAY, MIGHT, COULD

1 AFFIRMATIVE AND NEGATIVE STATEMENTS

Use the cues to complete this journal entry.

Thursday, July 3

I was supposed to go to the beach tomorrow, but they say it

_____might rain_____. I don't know what I'll do. I
　　　　1. (might / rain)

_____ shopping at the mall, instead. It's a
　　2. (may / go)

holiday weekend, so there _____ some good sales.
　　　　　　　　3. (could / be)

Maybe I'll call Julie. She _____ to go with me.
　　　　　　　　4. (might / want)

On second thought, she _____ home. She often
　　　　　　　5. (may / be)

goes away on holiday weekends. I don't know. Shopping

_____ such a good idea. The stores will probably
　　　6. (might / be)

be really crowded. I _____ to a movie. There's a
　　　　　　　7. (could / go)

Spanish movie at Cinema 8. I'm not sure. I'm afraid I

_____ enough of it. My Spanish really isn't that
　　8. (might / understand)

good. Maybe I'll call Ed and ask him if he wants to take a drive to see Aunt

Marla and Uncle Phil. He _____ go. He
　　　　　　　　9. (might / want to)

doesn't like driving in the rain. Oh well, I _____
　　　　　　　　　　10. (could / stay)

home and read a good book.

② CONTRAST: *BE GOING TO* OR *MIGHT*

Read these conversations. Complete the summary sentences with **be going to** *or* **might** *and the verbs in the box.*

buy	go	rain	see	work
call	have	read	~~visit~~	write

1. **LINDA:** Hello, Julie? This is Linda. Do you want to go to the mall with me?

   JULIE: I don't know. I'm thinking about going to my parents'. I'm not sure. Can I call you back?

   Julie _____ *might visit* _____ her parents.

2. **JULIE:** What are you looking for at the mall?

   LINDA: I need to get a new suit for work. I hope I can find one.

   Linda _____ a suit.

3. **LINDA:** Do you think we'll get some rain?

   CARL: Definitely. Look at those clouds.

   Carl thinks it _____.

4. **LINDA:** What are you doing today?

   CARL: I have tickets for a play.

   Carl _____ a play.

5. **LINDA:** What are you doing this weekend?

   SUE: I'm not sure. I'm thinking about taking a drive to the country. It depends on the weather.

   Sue _____ for a ride.

6. **LINDA:** Say, Ed. Do you want to see Aunt Marla and Uncle Phil tomorrow?

   ED: I can't. I have to go into the office this weekend.

   Ed _____ this weekend.

7. **LINDA:** How about dinner Saturday night?

   ED: That's an idea. Can I call and let you know tomorrow?

   Linda and Ed _____ dinner together.

8. **LINDA:** Hi, Aunt Marla. How are you?

   MARLA: Linda! How are you? It's good to hear your voice. Listen, we just started

   dinner. Can I call you back?

   LINDA: Sure.

   MARLA: OK. I'll speak to you soon.

   Marla _____ Linda.

9. **MARLA:** This is Aunt Marla. Sorry about before. What are you doing home on a

   holiday weekend?

   LINDA: I'm tired. I just want to stay home with a good book.

   Linda _____ a book.

10. **MARLA:** Do you have any other plans?

    LINDA: Maybe I'll catch up on some of my correspondence.

    Linda _____ some letters.

③ EDITING

Read Linda's letter. Find and correct four mistakes in the use of modals to express future possibility. The first mistake is already corrected.

> Dear Roberta,
>
> How are you? It's the Fourth of July, and it's raining really hard. They say it
> might OR may
> could clear up later. Then again, it ~~could~~ not. You never know with the weather.
>
> Do you remember my brother, Ed? He says hi. He might has dinner with me on
> Saturday night. We may go to a new Mexican restaurant that opened in the mall.
>
> I definitely might take some vacation next month. Perhaps we could do something
> together. It might not be fun to do some traveling. What do you think? Let me
> know.
>
> Love,
>
> Linda

4 PERSONALIZATION

Make a short "To Do" list for next weekend. Put a question mark (?)
next to the things you aren't sure you'll do.

To Do

1.

2.

3.

4.

5.

6.

7.

8.

---

*Now write sentences about what you **are going to do** and what you*
might do.

1. _____

2. _____

3. _____

4. _____

5. _____

6. _____

7. _____

8. _____

ASSUMPTIONS: MUST, HAVE (GOT) TO, MAY, MIGHT, COULD, CAN'T

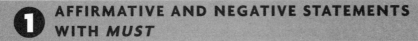

1 AFFIRMATIVE AND NEGATIVE STATEMENTS WITH *MUST*

Read the facts. Complete the conclusions with **must** *or* **must not**.

1. Jack is wearing a gold wedding band on his ring finger.

   He _____must be_____ married.
   (be)

2. You have been calling Alicia since 8:00 P.M., but no one answers the

   phone.

   She _____ at home.
   (be)

3. Jackie got 98 percent on her math test.

   Her parents _____ proud of her.
   (feel)

4. Carlos works from 9:00 to 5:00 and then attends night school.

   He _____ a lot of free time.
   (have)

5. Martin works as a mechanic in Al's Automobile Shop.

   He _____ a lot about cars.
   (know)

6. Monica owns two houses and four cars.

   She _____ a lot of money.
   (have)

7. Mr. Cantor always asks me to repeat what I say.

   He _____ well.
   (hear)

8. Chen only got four hours of sleep last night.

   He _____ very tired today.
   (feel)

153

(continued on next page)

9. Carmen was born in Mexico and moved to the United States when she was ten.

   She _____ Spanish.
   (speak)

10. Mindy never gets good grades.

    She _____ enough.
    (study)

11. Dan just bought a bottle of aspirin and four boxes of tissues.

    He _____ a cold.
    (have)

12. Ana and Giorgio didn't have any of the steak.

    They _____ meat.
    (eat)

❷ CONTRAST: *MUST OR MAY / MIGHT / COULD*

Circle the correct words to complete these conversations.

1. **A:** Someone broke into the Petersons' house.

   B: That's terrible! What did they take?

   A: All of Mrs. Peterson's jewelry.

   B: Oh, no. She could / (must) feel awful.

2. **A:** Is she home now?

   B: I don't know. She might / must be home. She sometimes gets home by 6:00.

3. **A:** Do the Petersons have insurance?

   B: Oh, they could / must. Mr. Peterson works at an insurance company.

4. **A:** Have you checked our burglar alarm lately?

   B: Yes. And I just put in a new battery.

   A: Good. So it must / might be OK.

5. **A:** Do you remember that guy we saw outside the Petersons' home last week?

   B: Yes. Why? Do you think he might / must be the burglar?

6. **A:** I don't know. I guess he must / could be the burglar. He looked a little suspicious.

   B: Maybe we should tell the police about him.

7. **A:** Someone's at the door.

   B: Who <u>could / must</u> it be?

   A: I don't know.

8. **A:** Detective Kramer wanted to ask us some questions about the burglary.

   B: Oh. It <u>must / could</u> be him. We're not expecting anybody else.

9. **A:** How old do you think Detective Kramer is?

   B: Well, he's been a detective for ten years. So he <u>must / might</u> be at least thirty-five.

10. **A:** You're right. He <u>couldn't / might not</u> be much younger than thirty-five. He probably started out as a police officer and became a detective in his early twenties.

   B: He looks a lot younger, though.

❸ SHORT ANSWERS WITH *MUST* OR *MAY / MIGHT / COULD*

Answer the questions. Include **be** *when necessary.*

1. **A:** Is Ron a detective?

   B: _____ *He might be* _____. He always carries a notepad.

2. **A:** Does Marta speak Spanish?

   B: _____. She lived in Spain for four years.

3. **A:** Do the Taylors have a lot of money?

   B: _____. They have two homes, and they're always taking expensive vacations.

4. **A:** Is Ricardo married?

   B: _____. He wears a wedding ring.

5. **A:** Does Anna know Meng?

   B: _____. They both work for the same company, but there are more than 100 employees.

6. **A:** Is your phone out of order?

   B: _____. It hasn't rung once today, and John always calls me by this time.

(continued on next page)

7. **A:** Are Marcia and Scott married?

   B: _____. They both have the same last name, but it's

   possible that they're brother and sister.

8. **A:** Does Glenda drive?

   B: _____. She owns a car.

9. **A:** Is Oscar an only child?

   B: _____. He's never mentioned a brother or sister. I really

   don't know.

10. **A:** Are the Hendersons away?

   B: _____. I haven't seen them for a week, and there are no

   lights on in their apartment.

---

4 CONTRAST: *MUST, COULD, CAN'T, COULDN'T, MIGHT NOT*

Read the description of a burglary suspect and look at the four pictures.
Complete the conversation with the correct words and the names of the
men in the pictures.

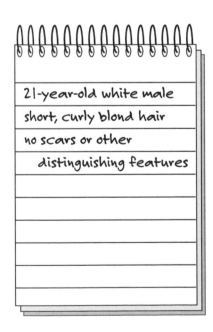

21-year-old white male
short, curly blond hair
no scars or other
   distinguishing features

Allen

Bob

Chet

Dave

DETECTIVE: Look at these four photos. It's possible that one of them

_____could_____ be the man we're looking for. Take your time.
　　　　　　1. (must / could)

WITNESS 1: Hhmm. What do you think? _____ it be this man?
　　　　　　　　　　　　　　　　　　2. (Could / Must)

WITNESS 2: It _____ be _____. He
　　　　　　3. (can't / must)　　　　　　　4. (Name)

has a scar on his face. What about _____? He has
　　　　　　　　　　　　　　　　5. (Name)

short blond hair and looks twenty-one.

WITNESS 1: I'm not sure. It _____ be. But it
　　　　　　　　6. (could / must)

_____ also be_____. He
　　　7. (might / must)　　　　　　　　　　　8. (Name)

also has blond hair and looks twenty-one.

WITNESS 2: But he has long hair.

WITNESS 1: The photo _____ be old. Maybe he cut it.
　　　　　　　　　　9. (could / couldn't)

WITNESS 2: That's true. Well, it definitely _____ be
　　　　　　　　　　　　　　　10. (couldn't / might not)

_____. He's too old. Maybe we could look at some
　　　11. (Name)

more photos.

---

⑤ PERSONALIZATION

Read the description of the burglar in Exercise 4. Look at these pictures.
Is one of them the burglar? What's your opinion? Complete the
sentences.

Ed　　　　　　Frank　　　　　　George

1. It could be _____ because _____.

2. It couldn't be _____ because _____.

3. It might be _____ because _____.

6 **EDITING**

Read this woman's journal entry. Find and correct six mistakes in the use of modals to express assumptions. The first mistake is already corrected.

> Just got home. It's really cold outside. The temperature ~~could~~ **must** be below freezing because the walkway is all covered with ice. What a day! We went down to the police station to look at photos. They must having hundreds of photos. They kept showing us more and more. We kept looking, but it was difficult to be sure. After all, we only saw the burglar for a few seconds. They've gotta have other witnesses besides us! There were a lot of people at the mall that day. We may not be the only ones who got a look at the burglar! That's the one thing I'm certain of! In spite of our uncertainty with the photos, the detective was very patient. I guess he must be used to witnesses like us. Nevertheless, it have to be frustrating for him. I know the police may really want to catch this guy.

NOUNS AND QUANTIFIERS

1 KINDS OF NOUNS

Put these nouns into the correct category.

~~biology~~	chair	class	country	day	dollar
Election Day	furniture	hamburger	honesty	ink	Japanese
money	news	pen	president	rice	Richard
snow	snowflake	spaghetti	story	sugar	swimming
Yeltsin	zoo				

Proper Nouns

_____   _____

_____   _____

Common Nouns

Count   **Non-Count**

_____   ___biology___

_____   _____

_____   _____

_____   _____

_____   _____

_____   _____

_____   _____

_____   _____

_____   _____

_____   _____

_____   _____

_____   _____

② COUNT AND NON-COUNT NOUNS

Complete these food facts. Use the correct form of the words in parentheses ( ).

1. ____Chocolate____ ____has____ a chemical that creates a feeling similar to being in
   (Chocolate)   (have)
   love.

2. _____ _____ the most popular food in the United States.
   (Potato)   (be)
   _____ _____ the most popular food in the world.
   (Rice)   (be)

3. _____ _____ Americans' favorite snack food.
   (Potato chip)   (be)

4. _____ _____ more potato chips than any other _____
   (American)   (eat)   (people)
   in the world.

5. Chewing raw onions for five minutes _____ all the germs in your mouth.
   (kill)

6. _____ _____ at least 5,000 years old.
   (Popcorn)   (be)

7. _____ _____ really nuts. They are members of the bean family.
   (Peanut)   (not be)

8. _____ _____ been around for just a little over a hundred years.
   (Peanut butter)   (have)
   It's a relatively new health-food invention.

9. The _____ of the hot dog _____ very long. It began 3,500 years
   (history)   (be)
   ago.

10. _____ _____ the favorite dessert in the United States.
    (Ice cream)   (be)

③ MUCH OR MANY

*Complete this food quiz. Use **much** or **many**. Then try to guess the answer to the questions. Circle the letter of your choice.*

1. How ____much____ Vitamin C does an onion have? As ____much____ as

   a. two apples

   b. one orange

   c. three carrots

2. How _____ rolls are there in a "baker's dozen"?

   a. eleven

   b. twelve

   c. thirteen

3. How _____ pizza does the average person from the United States eat each

year?

   a. 13 pounds

   b. 23 pounds

   c. 33 pounds

4. In how _____ countries can you find a McDonalds' fast-food restaurant?

   a. almost 50

   b. almost 80

   c. almost 120

5. How _____ chocolate does the average person in Switzerland eat each year?

   a. 10.7 pounds

   b. 20.7 pounds

   c. 30.7 pounds

6. How _____ calories are there in a cup of regular vanilla ice cream?

   a. 170

   b. 270

   c. 370

7. How _____ ice cream does the average person in Finland eat each year?

   a. 22 pints

   b. 38 pints

   c. 46 pints

8. How _____ weeks is it safe to keep butter in the refrigerator?

   a. four

   b. six

   c. eight

4 QUANTIFIERS

Circle the correct words to complete the conversation.

A: How was the party?

B: It was good. I saw (a lot of)/ much people from my childhood.
   1.

A: That's nice. Were there <u>many / much</u> family members there too?
   2.

B: No. Unfortunately <u>a few / few</u> relatives live nearby, so not <u>many / much</u> could come.
   3.   **4.**

A: How was the food?

B: Delicious! In fact, there's so <u>many / much</u> left over, you should come by tonight. I can
   5.

show you the photos too. <u>Several / A great deal of</u> people had cameras with them, and
   6.

we got <u>some / a little</u> pictures back already.
   7.

A: That was fast!

B: Yeah. We brought them to one of those places where you only have to wait <u>a few / few</u>
   8.

hours to get them back.

A: Great! What time should I come over?

B: Let's see. I get out of school at 5:00, and I don't think I'll have <u>a little / much</u> homework
   9.

tonight. How about 7:00?

A: Will that give you <u>enough / many</u> time to get ready?
   10.

B: Sure. There's really nothing to do.

A: OK. See you then.

5 PERSONALIZATION

*Describe a party or another social event you've attended. Who was
there? What kind of food was served at the event?*

_____

_____

_____

_____

_____

ARTICLES: INDEFINITE AND DEFINITE

1 INDEFINITE AND DEFINITE ARTICLES

Circle the correct choice to complete these conversations that take place in school. If you don't need an article, circle Ø.

1. **A:** Can I borrow **a** / the pen?

   B: Sure. Take <u>a / the</u> one on <u>a / the</u> desk. I don't need it.

2. **A:** Is <u>a / the</u> teacher here yet?

   B: No, she hasn't come yet.

3. **A:** What do you think of Mr. Mencz?

   B: He's <u>a / the</u> best teacher I've ever had.

4. **A:** Have you done <u>the / Ø</u> homework?

   B: Yes. But I don't think I got <u>a / the</u> last answer right.

5. **A:** Could you open <u>a / the</u> window, please?

   B: Which one?

   A: <u>A / The</u> one next to <u>a / the</u> door.

   B: Sure.

6. **A:** Who's that?

   B: That's <u>a / the</u> school principal.

   A: Oh, I've never seen her before.

7. **A:** Do you like <u>the / Ø</u> history?

   B: It's OK. But I prefer <u>the / Ø</u> science.

8. **A:** We learned about <u>an / the</u> ozone layer in science class yesterday.

   B: Did you know there's <u>a / the</u> hole in it?

   A: Yeah. It's pretty scary.

(continued on next page)

9. **A:** What kind of work do you do?

   B: I'm <u>an / the</u> engineer. What about you?

   A: I'm <u>a / Ø</u> mechanic.

10. **A:** Are they <u>some / Ø</u> students?

   B: I don't think so. They look like <u>the / Ø</u> teachers.

11. **A:** Do you know where I can get <u>some / the</u> water around here?

   B: Sure. There's <u>a / the</u> water fountain right across <u>a / the</u> hall, right next to <u>the / Ø</u> rest rooms.

12. **A:** Do you know what <u>a / the</u> homework is for tomorrow?

   B: We have to read <u>a / the</u> fable.

   A: Which one?

   B: <u>A / The</u> one on page 23.

2   INDEFINITE AND DEFINITE ARTICLES

Complete the conversation. Use **a / an** *or* **the** *when necessary.*

BING YANG: Hi, Georgina. What are you doing?

GEORGINA: I'm reading _____*a*_____ fable for my English class.
                      1.

BING YANG: What's _____ fable? I've never heard the word before.
                    2.

GEORGINA: _____ fable is _____ short story about _____
           3.   **4.**   **5.**
              animals.

BING YANG: About _____ animals? Like _____ science story?
                    6.   **7.**

GEORGINA: No. It's _____ fiction. _____ animals act like
                  8.   **9.**
            _____ people. They usually teach _____ lesson.
           10.   **11.**
            _____ lesson is called _____ moral of _____
           12.   **13.**   **14.**
            story, and it always comes at _____ end.
                               15.

BING YANG: That's interesting. Who's _____ author of _____ fable
                                  16.   **17.**
            you're reading?

GEORGINA: Aesop. He was _____ ancient Greek writer.
                   18.

BING YANG: Oh, now I know what you're talking about. My parents used to read

_____ fables to me when I was _____ child.
　　　　　　19.　　　　　　　　　　　　　　　　　　20.

GEORGINA: Well, they're also good for _____ adults. I'll lend you
　　　　　　　　　　　　　　　　　　　　　21.

_____ book when I'm finished if you're interested.
　　22.

BING YANG: Thanks. I am.

❸ INDEFINITE AND DEFINITE ARTICLES

Complete this version of an Aesop's fable. Use **a / an** *or* **the** *when necessary.*

The Fox and the Goat

_____A_____ fox fell into _____ well and couldn't get out again. Finally,
　　1.　　　　　　　　　　　　　　2.

_____ thirsty goat came by and saw _____ fox in _____
　　3.　　　　　　　　　　　　　　　　　　　　　　　4.　　　　　　　　　　　5.

well. "Is _____ water good?" _____ goat asked. "Good?" said
　　　　　6.　　　　　　　　　　　　　　7.

_____ fox. "It's _____ best water I've ever tasted in my whole life.
　　8.　　　　　　　　　　9.

Why don't you come down and try it?"

_____ goat was very thirsty, so he jumped into _____ well. When
　　10.　　　　　　　　　　　　　　　　　　　　　　　　　　11.

he was finished drinking, he looked for _____ way to get out of
　　　　　　　　　　　　　　　　　　　　　12.

_____ well, but, of course, there wasn't any. Then _____ fox said, "I
　　13.　　　　　　　　　　　　　　　　　　　　　　　　14.

have _____ excellent idea. Stand on your back legs and place your front legs
　　　　15.

firmly against _____ front side of _____ well. Then, I'll climb onto
　　　　　　　16.　　　　　　　　　　　　　　　17.

(continued on next page)

your back and, from there, I'll step on your horns and be able to get out. When I'm out, I'll

help you get out, too." _____ goat thought this was _____ good idea
                                    18.   **19.**
and followed _____ advice.
                        20.

    When _____ fox was out of _____ well, he quickly and quietly
                            21.   **22.**
walked away. _____ goat called loudly after him and reminded him of
                        23.

_____ promise he had made to help him out. But _____ fox turned
24.   **25.**
and said, "You should have as much sense in your head as you have _____
                                                                            26.
hairs in your beard. You jumped into _____ well before making sure you
                                            27.
could get out again."

    Moral: Look before you leap.

ANSWER KEY

Where the full form is given, the contraction is also acceptable. Where the contracted form is given, the full form is also acceptable.

PART | PRESENT, PAST, AND FUTURE: REVIEW AND EXPANSION

UNIT **PRESENT PROGRESSIVE AND SIMPLE PRESENT TENSE**

2. getting, gets
3. trying, tries
4. planning, plans
5. having, has
6. doing, does
7. matching, matches
8. grabbing, grabs
9. giving, gives
10. saying, says

2

2. drives
3. takes
4. isn't taking
5. is taking
6. are repairing
7. is using
8. doesn't . . . use
9. takes
10. moves
11. is slowing down
12. 's raining
13. doesn't like
14. drives
15. is listening
16. listens
17. is describing
18. doesn't want
19. isn't moving
20. hates
21. feels
22. knows
23. wishes

3

(Answers will vary.)

4

Postcard 1
2. is shining
3. is blowing
4. feels
5. know
6. are flying
7. are building

Postcard 2
1. are traveling
2. 'm standing
3. is getting
4. looks
5. has
6. 's taking
7. 's starting

Postcard 3
1. 'm studying
2. living
3. is improving
4. speak
5. 're helping
6. want
7. miss

5

3. Mario and Silvia OR They go to school.
4. Mario and Silvia OR They are having lunch.
5. Mario studies at the library. Silvia plays basketball.
6. Mario goes home. Silvia visits her grandmother.
7. Mario and Silvia OR They are doing (their) homework.
8. Mario has dinner. Silvia practices the guitar.
9. Mario plays computer games. Silvia makes dinner.
10. Mario is reading the newspaper. Silvia is washing the dishes.

6

2. He doesn't listen to the radio. He watches TV.
3. Silvia doesn't visit her grandfather. She visits her grandmother.
4. She isn't practicing the piano. She's practicing the guitar.
5. He doesn't watch the news. He reads the newspaper.

7

2. **A:** When do Mario and Silvia get up?
   B: They get up at 7:30.
3. **A:** Does Silvia watch TV in the morning?
   B: No, she doesn't.
4. **A:** What are they doing now?
   B: They're having lunch.
5. **A:** Is Mario studying at the library now?
   B: No, he isn't.
6. **A:** Does he do his homework at school?
   B: No, he doesn't.
7. **A:** When does Silvia play basketball?
   B: She plays basketball at 3:00.
8. **A:** Does Mario play computer games before dinner?
   B: No, he doesn't.

8

2. Silvia is usually on time.
3. Silvia and Mario never miss school.
4. These days they're studying English. OR They're studying English these days.
5. They usually speak Italian.
6. Now they're speaking English. OR They're speaking English now.
7. Silvia and Mario always do their homework.
8. Mario is often tired.
9. The students usually eat lunch in school.
10. They're always hungry.
11. At the moment Silvia is having a snack. OR Silvia is having a snack at the moment.
12. Silvia rarely goes to bed late.

9

Hi, How are you? I **'m writing** ~~write~~ you this letter on the bus. I hope you can read my writing. They **'re doing** ~~do~~ some repairs on the road, so it's bumpy and the bus **is shaking** ~~shakes~~. Guess what? I am **have** ~~having~~ a job as a clerk in the mail room of a small company. The pay isn't good, but I **I like** ~~'m liking~~ the people there. They're all friendly, and we **speak** ~~are speaking~~ Spanish all the time. I'm also taking Spanish classes at night at a language institute. The class **meets** ~~is meeting~~

three times a week. It just started last week, so **I don't know** I'm ~~not knowing~~ many of the other students yet. They seem nice, though.

I think I'm ~~thinking~~ that I'm beginning to get accustomed to living here. At first I experienced some "culture shock." I understand that this is quite normal. But these days I **'m meeting** ~~meet~~ more and more people because of my job and my class, so I'm feeling more connected to things.

What **are you doing** ~~do you do~~ these days? **Are you still looking** ~~Do you still look~~ for a new job?

Please write when you can. I always like to hear from you.

UNIT 2 IMPERATIVE

1

2. Look down.
3. Don't lean backward.
4. Take a small step.
5. Don't breathe in.
6. Count slowly.
7. Don't speak loudly.
8. Keep your eyes shut.
9. Don't wear tight clothes.
10. Wear light clothes.
11. Don't turn the lights off.
12. Turn the music up.
13. Put the heat on low.
14. Don't come late.

2

3. Walk
4. ride
5. Go
6. Don't turn
7. make
8. Continue
9. stop
10. Don't cross
11. be
12. Don't pass
13. Have
14. Don't work

3

Your mother called. **Call** ~~Calls~~ her at your sister's tonight.

Don't ~~you~~ call after 10:00, though.

I went to the gym.

Please *
Wash ~~please~~ the dishes and ~~threw~~ **throw** out the trash.

take
If anyone calls for me, ~~takes~~ a message.

Thanks a lot.

* OTHER POSSIBLE CORRECTIONS: Wash the dishes, please, and throw out the trash. OR Wash the dishes and throw out the trash, please.

④

(Answers will vary.)

UNIT SIMPLE PAST TENSE

❶

3. caught	15. needed
4. did	16. opened
5. looked	17. put
6. found	18. read
7. gave	19. said
8. hurried	20. thought
9. saw	21. understood
10. died	22. voted
11. kissed	23. won
12. came	24. felt
13. lived	25. was . . . were
14. met	

❷

2. was	7. wasn't . . . was
3. weren't . . . were	8. was . . . wasn't
4. wasn't	9. were
5. was	10. were
6. wasn't . . . was	

❸

2. A: Where was Simone de Beauvoir from?
   B: She was from France.
3. A: What nationality was Pablo Neruda?
   B: He was Chilean.
4. A: Who was Boccaccio?
   B: He was a poet and storyteller.
5. A: Was Agatha Christie French?
   B: No, she wasn't.
6. A: What nationality was Lorraine Hansberry?
   B: She was American.
7. A: Was Honoré de Balzac a poet?
   B: No, he wasn't.
8. A: When was Karel Čapek born?
   B: He was born in 1890.
9. A: Who was Isaak Babel?
   B: He was a short-story writer and playwright.

④

Biography 1
2. spent
3. wrote
4. included
5. translated
6. died
Biography 2
1. was
2. lived
3. began
4. called
5. had
6. painted
Biography 3
1. were
2. built
3. flew
4. watched
5. took place
6. lasted

❺

2. A: What did he do?
   B: He was a writer. OR He wrote books and translated other people's works.
3. A: Did he write poetry?
   B: No, he didn't.
4. A: Where did he spend most of his life?
   B: (He spent most of his life) in the United States.
5. A: What did people call Anna Mary Robertson Moses?
   B: (They called her) Grandma Moses.
6. A: What did she do?
   B: She was a painter. OR She painted.
7. A: When did she begin painting?
   B: She began painting in her seventies.
8. A: Did she have formal art training?
   B: No, she didn't.
9. A: Where did the Wright brothers build their first planes?
   B: (They built their first planes) in their bicycle shop in Ohio.
10. A: Did both brothers fly the *Flyer 1*?
    B: No, they didn't.
11. A: Where did the first controlled flight take place?
    B: (It took place) near Kitty Hawk, North Carolina.
12. A: How long did the flight last?
    B: (It lasted) only about 12 seconds.

❻

3. Orville didn't have serious health problems.
4. Wilbur didn't grow a moustache.
5. Orville didn't lose most of his hair.
6. Wilbur didn't take courses in Latin.

7. Wilbur didn't like to play jokes.
8. Wilbur didn't dress very fashionably.
9. Wilbur didn't play the guitar.
10. Orville didn't build the first glider.
11. Orville didn't make the first attempts to fly.
12. Orville didn't choose the location of Kitty Hawk.
13. Wilbur didn't have a lot of patience.
14. Wilbur didn't live a long life.

7

Pablo Neruda (1904–1973) Pablo Neruda ~~were~~ *was* a famous poet, political activist, and diplomat. He was born in Parral, Chile. When he was seventeen, he ~~gone~~ *went* to Santiago to continue his education. He did not ~~finished~~ *finish*, but he soon published his first book. Neruda ~~spends~~ *spent* the next several decades traveling and continuing to write poetry. In 1971, while he was Chile's ambassador to France, he ~~winned~~ *won* the Nobel Prize in literature. He ~~dead~~ *died* two years later.

UNIT 4 USED TO

1

2. People used to read
3. People used to cook
4. People used to fly
5. People used to have
6. People used to wash
7. People used to use
8. It used to take

2

2. didn't use to work
3. didn't use to have
4. used to take
5. didn't use to be
6. used to live
7. didn't use to like
8. didn't use to know
9. used to return
10. used to write

3

2. **A:** Where did she use to live?
   B: She used to live in New York.

3. **A:** What did she use to do?
   B: She used to be a student.
4. **A:** Did she use to have long hair?
   B: Yes, she did.
5. **A:** Did she use to wear glasses?
   B: No, she didn't.
6. **A:** Did she use to be married?
   B: Yes, she did.
7. **A:** Did she use to use *Ms.* before her name?
   B: No, she didn't.

4

Today I ran into an old classmate. At first, I almost didn't recognize him! He looked so different. He used to ~~had~~ *have* very dark hair. Now he's almost all gray. He also used to ~~being~~ *be* a little heavy. Now he's quite thin. And he was wearing a suit and tie! I couldn't believe it. He never ~~use~~ *used* to dress that way. He only used to wear jeans! His personality seemed different, too. He didn't ~~used~~ *use* to talk very much. Now he seems very outgoing.

I wonder what he thought about me! I'm sure I look and act a lot different from the way I ~~was~~ used to too!

5

(Answers will vary.)

UNIT 5 PAST PROGRESSIVE AND SIMPLE PAST TENSE

1

2. wasn't writing
3. was answering
4. were eating
5. weren't eating
6. was attending
7. weren't writing
8. were discussing
9. wasn't answering
10. was returning

2

2. **A:** What was he doing at 9:30?
   B: He was meeting with Ms. Jacobs.
3. **A:** Was Mr. Cotter writing police reports at 10:30?
   B: No, he wasn't.

4. **A:** What kind of reports was he writing?
   B: He was writing financial reports.
5. **A:** What was he doing at 11:30?
   B: He was answering correspondence.
6. **A:** Was he having lunch at 12:00?
   B: Yes, he was.
7. **A:** Who was eating lunch with him?
   B: Mr. Webb was eating lunch with him.
8. **A:** Where were they having lunch?
   B: They were having lunch at Sol's Cafe.
9. **A:** Who was he talking to at 3:30?
   B: He was talking to Alan.
10. **A:** What were they discussing?
    B: They were discussing the budget.

❸

3. were visiting
4. took place
5. killed
6. injured
7. took
8. exploded
9. went out
10. stopped
11. started
12. were eating
13. shook
14. occurred
15. crumbled
16. collapsed
17. arrived
18. found
19. was walking
20. went off
21. had
22. were carrying
23. were riding
24. went out
25. stopped
26. had to
27. reached
28. was waiting
29. drove
30. was happening

❹

2. What happened when the bomb exploded?
3. What were the schoolchildren doing when the lights went out?
4. How many people were working in the building when the bomb exploded?
5. What were they doing when the bomb went off?
6. What happened to the offices when the blast occurred?
7. What was he doing when the bomb exploded?
8. What happened when the rescue workers brought him to the ambulance?

UNIT FUTURE

❶

2. She's going to wash the car.
3. They're going to get gas.
4. She's going to make a left turn.
5. She's going to get a ticket.
6. They're going to crash.
7. They're going to eat lunch.
8. It's going to rain.

❷

2. How long are you going to stay?
3. Are you going to stay at a hotel?
4. What are you going to do in San Francisco?
5. Are you going to visit Fisherman's Wharf?
6. Is your daughter going to go with you?
7. What is he going to do?
8. When are you going to leave?

❸

2. He isn't going to take the train. He's going to fly OR take a plane.
3. He isn't going to travel alone. He's going to travel with his wife.
4. They aren't going to leave from Chicago. They're going to leave from New York.
5. They aren't going to fly US Airways. They're going to fly FairAirs.
6. They aren't going to leave on July 11. They're going to leave on June 11.
7. It isn't going to depart at 7:00 A.M. It's going to depart at 7:00 P.M.
8. They aren't going to sit apart. They're going to sit together.
9. They aren't going to be in a smoking section. They're going to be in a non-smoking OR no smoking section.
10. She isn't going to sit in seat 15B. She's going to sit in seat 15C.

❹

2. will
3. will become
4. Will . . . replace
5. won't replace
6. will . . . operate
7. will . . . do
8. 'll be
9. 'll sing
10. 'll dance
11. Will . . . tell
12. will
13. won't . . . be
14. will . . . do
15. Will . . . have
16. will
17. will . . . help
18. won't replace
19. 'll perform
20. won't be
21. will improve
22. will lose
23. will create
24. Will . . . need
25. will . . . look
26. won't look
27. 'll resemble
28. will . . . happen
29. 'll happen

❺

Next Wednesday <u>is</u> the first performance of *Bats*. Melissa Robins <u>is playing</u> the leading role. Robins, who lives in Italy and who is vacationing in Greece, is not available for an interview at this time. She <u>is</u>, however, <u>appearing</u> on Channel 8's "Theater Talk" sometime next month.

Although shows traditionally begin at 8:00 P.M., *Bats*, because of its length, <u>starts</u> a half hour earlier.

Immediately following the opening-night performance, the company <u>is having</u> a reception in the theater lounge. Tickets are still available. Call 555-6310 for more information.

2. I'm going to do
3. I'll ask
4. it's going to rain
5. are they showing
6. we're going to have
7. I'll take
8. We're going to arrive
9. are we going to get
10. We'll take
11. We're landing
12. are you going to stay

'm
I ~~going~~ to stay here for a week with my parents.

We have a lot of fun things planned.
we're seeing OR we're going to see
Tomorrow night we'll see a play called *Bats*. Mom

already bought tickets for it. The play begins at
're having OR we're going to have
8:00, and before that we ~~have~~ dinner on

Fisherman's Wharf. Right now we're sitting in

Golden Gate Park, but we have to leave. It has
's going to
suddenly gotten very cloudy. It ~~will~~ rain!
'll call
I ~~call~~ you soon.

Jason

UNIT 7 FUTURE TIME CLAUSES

1

2. is . . . 'll drink (c)
3. finish . . . 'll do (g)
4. washes . . . 'll dry (e)
5. get in . . . 'll fasten (d)
6. gets . . . 'll drive (b)
7. stops . . . 'll need (f)
8. is . . . 'll be (a)

2

2. will apply . . . before . . . finishes
3. After . . . finishes . . . 'll visit
4. While . . . works . . . 'll take
5. 'll visit . . . before . . . gets
6. When . . . finishes . . . 'll fly
7. 'll get married . . . when . . . 's
8. 'll return . . . after . . . gets married

3

2. retire
3. will . . . go
4. have
5. turn
6. will want
7. visit
8. won't want

4

2. Vera saves enough money from her summer job, she's going to buy a plane ticket.
3. Vera goes home, she's going to buy presents for her family.
4. Vera arrives at the airport, her father will be there to drive her home.
5. Vera and her father get home, they'll have dinner.
6. Vera will give her family the presents . . . they finish dinner.
7. Vera's brother will wash the dishes . . . Vera's sister dries them.
8. The whole family will stay up talking . . . the clock strikes midnight.
9. they go to bed, they'll all feel very tired.
10. Vera will fall asleep . . . her head hits the pillow.

5

(Answers will vary.)

UNIT 8 WH- QUESTIONS: SUBJECT AND PREDICATE

1

2. Whose phone rang at midnight?
3. Who was calling for Michelle?
4. Who was having a party?
5. How many people left the party?
6. What surprised them?
7. Whose friend called the police?
8. How many police arrived?
9. What happened next?
10. Who told the police about a theft?
11. Whose jewelry disappeared?
12. How many necklaces vanished?

2

2. How many rooms does her apartment have? (f)
3. How much rent does she pay? (j)
4. When does she pay the rent? (c)
5. Who(m) does she live with? (h)
6. What does she do? (g)
7. Which company does she work for? (d)

8. How long does she plan to stay there? (a)
9. How does she get to work? (b)
10. Why does she take the bus? (i)

3

2. Why did you leave Chicago?
3. Who moved with you?
4. Where did you get a job?
5. When did it start?
6. How many rooms does it have?
7. How many of the rooms came with carpeting?
8. How much do you each pay?
9. What do you need to buy?
10. Whose brother wants to visit her?
11. Who called last Sunday?
12. Who(m) did you speak to?
13. When do they want to visit you?
14. Why is there plenty of room?

PART ‖ PRONOUNS AND PHRASAL VERBS

UNIT REFLEXIVE AND RECIPROCAL PRONOUNS

1

2. himself
3. themselves
4. itself
5. herself
6. yourself OR yourselves (yourselves OR yourself)
7. themselves
8. itself
9. themselves
10. ourselves

2

2. each other
3. herself
4. themselves
5. each other's
6. herself
7. yourselves
8. itself
9. ourselves
10. each other

3

2. are enjoying each other's
3. is going to help himself
4. are talking to themselves
5. are introducing themselves
6. are talking to each other
7. drove herself
8. blames OR is blaming himself
9. are criticizing one another OR each other
10. are thanking one another OR each other

4

I really enjoyed ~~me~~ *myself* at Gina's party! Hank was there and we talked to ~~ourselves~~ *each other OR one another* quite a bit. He's a little depressed about losing his job. He thinks it's all his own fault, and he blames ~~him~~ *himself* for the whole thing. Hank introduced ~~myself~~ *me* to several of his friends. I spoke a lot to this one woman, Cara. We have a lot of things in common, and after just an hour, we felt like we had known ~~each other's~~ *each other* forever. Cara, ~~himself~~ *herself*, is a computer programmer, just like me.

At first I was nervous about going to the party alone. I sometimes feel a little uncomfortable when I'm in a social situation by ~~oneself~~ *myself*. But this time was different. Before I went, I kept telling myself to relax. My roommate, too, kept telling ~~myself~~ *me*, "Don't be so hard on ~~you~~ *yourself*! Just have fun!" That's what I advised Hank to do, too. Before we left the party, Hank and I promised ~~us~~ *each other OR one another* to keep in touch. I hope to see him again soon.

UNIT PHRASAL VERBS

1

2. out	9. up
3. on	10. up
4. off	11. out
5. up	12. up
6. out	13. out
7. down	14. in
8. out	15. out

2

2. Pick out, help . . . out	6. Look . . . over
3. Look up	7. Do . . . over
4. Set up, talk over	8. Hand . . . in
5. Write up	

3

2. clean it up	6. turn it down
3. call her up	7. hand them in
4. turn it down	8. drop it off
5. wake him up	

2. Bring up the homework problems. OR Bring the homework problems up.
3. Point out common mistakes. OR Point common mistakes out.
4. Talk them over.
5. Go on to the next unit.
6. Call off Friday's class. OR Call Friday's class off.
7. Make up the final exam questions. OR Make the final exam questions up.
8. Hand them out.

How are things going? I'm already into the second month of the spring semester, and I've got a lot of work to do. For science class, I have to write a term paper. The professor made ^{up} ~~over~~ a list of possible topics. After looking ^{them over} ~~over them~~, I think I've picked one out. I'm going to write about chimpanzees. I've already gone to the library to look ^{up} some information ^{OR up} about them in the encyclopedia ~~up~~. I found ^{out} ~~up~~ some very interesting facts.

Did you know that their hands look very much like their feet, and that they have fingernails and toenails? Their thumbs and big toes are "opposable." This makes it easy for them to pick things ^{up} ~~out~~ with both their fingers and toes. Their arms are longer than their legs. This helps ^{them out} ~~out them~~ too, because they can reach out to fruit growing on thin branches that could not otherwise support their weight. Adult males weigh between 90 and 115 pounds, and they are about four feet high when they stand ^{up} ~~out~~.

Like humans, chimpanzees are very social. They travel in groups called "communities." Mothers bring ^{up} ~~out~~ their chimps, who stay with them until about the age of seven. Even after the chimps have grown up, there is still a lot of contact with other chimpanzees.

I could go on, but I need to stop writing now so I can clean ^{up} ~~out~~ my room (it's a mess!) a little before going to bed. It's late already, and I have to

get ^{up early} ~~early up~~ tomorrow morning for my 9:00 A.M. class.

Please write and let me know how you are. Or call ^{me up} ~~up me~~ sometime! It would be great to speak to you.

PART III MODALS AND RELATED VERBS AND EXPRESSIONS

UNIT II ABILITY: *CAN, COULD, BE ABLE TO*

3. can read an English newspaper . . . could (read one)
4. couldn't read an English novel . . . can't (read one).
5. can speak on the phone . . . couldn't (speak on the phone).
6. couldn't speak with a group of people . . . can (speak with a group of people).
7. couldn't write a social letter . . . can (write one).
8. Before the course he couldn't write a business letter, and he still can't (write one).
9. He can order a meal in English now, and he could (order a meal in English) before, too.
10. He can go shopping now, and he could (go shopping) before, too.
SUMMARY: Fernando can do a lot more now than he could (do) before the course.

2. A: What languages can you speak?
3. A: Could you speak Spanish when you were a child?
   B: No, I couldn't.
4. A: Could you speak French?
   B: Yes, I could.
5. A: Before you came here, could you understand spoken English?
   B: No, I couldn't.
6. A: Can you understand song lyrics?
   B: Yes, I can.
7. A: Before this course, could you write a business letter in English?
   B: No, I couldn't.
8. A: Could you drive a car before you came here?
   B: No, I couldn't.
9. A: Can you drive a car now?
   B: No, I can't.
10. A: Can you swim?
   B: Yes, I can.

11. **A:** Could you surf before you came here?
    B: No, I couldn't.
12. **A:** What can you do now that you couldn't do before?
    B: can do . . . couldn't do

2. are able to interpret
3. are not able to distinguish
4. are not able to understand
5. are able to hear
6. have been able to regain
7. are able to read
8. is not able to recognize
9. is not able to work
10. are able to communicate

4

2. **A:** Will she be able to hear
   B: Yes, she will.
3. **A:** Will she be able to hear
   B: No, she won't.
4. **A:** Will she be able to hear
   B: Yes, she will.
5. **A:** Will she be able to hear
   B: Yes, she will.

5

2. could read
3. could not OR couldn't accept
4. was able to learn
5. was able to accept
6. could see
7. will . . . be able to do
8. can do
9. can do
10. has been able to master
11. has been able to speak
12. will be able to get

6

Before I came to this country I ~~can't~~ **couldn't** do many things in English. For example, I couldn't follow a conversation if many people were talking at the same time. I remember one occasion at a party. I wasn't able ∧**to** understand a word! I felt so uncomfortable. Finally, my aunt came to pick me up, and I ~~could~~ **was able to** leave the party.

Today I can ~~to~~ understand much better. Since last month I ~~can~~ **have been able to** practice a lot. I am taking classes at the adult center. My teacher is very good. She can ~~explains~~ **explain** things well, and she

always gives us the chance to talk a lot in class. I can do a lot now, and I think in a few more months I ~~can~~ **'ll be able to** do even more.

 (the image marks the "7" section header)

(Answers will vary.)

U N I T 12 PERMISSION: MAY, COULD, CAN, DO YOU MIND IF . . . ?

1

2. c.   6. a.
3. b.   7. e.
4. h.   8. g.
5. f.

2

2. we (please) review Unit 6 (please)?
3. I (please) borrow your pen (please)?
4. I look at your (class) notes?
5. I come late to the next class?
6. my husband (please) come to the next class with me (please)?
7. I (please) ask a question (please)?
8. we (please) use a dictionary (please)?
9. we (please) leave five minutes early (please)?
10. my sister goes on the class trip with the rest of the class?

3

(Answers will vary.)

4

2. can bring   6. may not pay
3. can't OR cannot drink   7. may not purchase
4. can pay   8. can't OR cannot get
5. can pay

5

I've been sick for the past two days. That's why I missed the last test. May I ~~taking~~ **take** a make up exam?

Yes. If you bring a doctor's note.

Could my brother ~~comes~~ **come** to class and take notes for me on Tuesday?

Yes, he ~~could~~ can.

Do you mind ~~when~~ ^{if} he tapes the class for me?

Not at all. He's welcome to tape the class.

One last request—I know I missed some handouts. May I have ^{please} ~~please~~ copies of them?

Sure. I'll give them to your brother on

Tuesday.

Thanks a lot.

UNIT REQUESTS: WILL, WOULD, COULD, CAN, WOULD YOU MIND . . . ?

❶

2. a	**7.** b
3. h	**8.** i
4. g	**9.** f
5. j	**10.** e
6. c	

Requests granted: 2, 4, 5, 6, 7, 9, 10
Requests refused: 1, 3, 8

❷

2. opening the window
3. mail a letter
4. pick up a sandwich
5. staying late tonight
6. keep the noise down
7. come to my office
8. get Frank's phone number
9. explaining this note to me
10. lend me $5.00

❸

(Note 3) Will you return please the stapler? → Will you please return the stapler? OR Will you return the stapler, please?
(Note 5) Would you mind leave → Would you mind leaving
(Note 6) Could you please remember to lock the door. → Could you please remember to lock the door?
(Note 7) Would you please to call Ms. Rivera before the end of the day? → Would you please call Ms. Rivera before the end of the day? OR Would you call Ms. Rivera before the end of the day, please?
(Note 8) Also, would you mind to e-mail Lisa Barker a copy? → Also, would you mind e-mailing Lisa Barker a copy?

❹

(Answers will vary.)

UNIT ADVICE: SHOULD, OUGHT TO, HAD BETTER

❶

3. What should I wear?
4. Should I bring a gift?
5. No, you shouldn't.
6. Should I bring something to eat or drink?
7. You should bring something to drink.
8. When should I respond?
9. You should respond by May 15.
10. Should I call Aunt Rosa?
11. No, you shouldn't.
12. Who(m) should I call?
13. You should leave a message at 555-3234.

❷

2. You'd better tell
3. You'd better not leave
4. You'd better not arrive
5. You'd better write
6. You'd better dress
7. You'd better not chew
8. You'd better not call
9. You'd better not stare
10. You'd better not ask
11. You'd better thank
12. You'd better go
13. You'd better have

❸

2. you should OR ought to OR 'd better wear
3. Should I tell
4. You'd better OR ought to OR should wait
5. Should I offer
6. They should OR ought to pay OR You shouldn't pay
7. Should I write
8. should I send
9. You should OR ought to OR 'd better wait
10. I'd better not forget
11. Should I call
12. You'd better call

❹

   Congratulations on your graduation! Your aunt and I are very proud of you.

   I hear you are looking for a job. You know you really ~~oughta~~ ^{ought to OR should} speak to your cousin Mike. He's had a lot of experience in this area. You shouldn't ~~taking~~ ^{take} the first job they offer you. ~~You've~~ ^{You'd} better give yourself a lot of time to find something you'll enjoy. It's important to be happy with what you do.

Maybe you should speak to a job counselor. In any case, you ~~oughtn't~~ shouldn't rush into anything! Should I ask Mike to call you? He really should ~~gets~~ get in touch with you about this.

Well, that's enough advice for one letter.

(*Answers will vary.*)

UNIT SUGGESTIONS: *LET'S, COULD, WHY DON'T . . . ?, WHY NOT . . . ?, HOW ABOUT . . . ?*

1

2. a.
3. b.
4. g.
5. j.
6. e.
7. i.
8. f.
9. d.
10. h.

2

2. Maybe you could .
3. Let's .
4. How about ?
5. Why don't you ?
6. Let's .
7. Maybe we could .
8. Why don't you ?
9. How about ?
10. That's a good idea .

3

2. take the "T"
3. go to Haymarket
4. taking an elevator to the top of the John Hancock Observatory
5. take a boat excursion
6. going to the New England Aquarium
7. eat at Legal Seafoods
8. walk along the waterfront
9. going shopping in Downtown Crossing
10. walk the Freedom Trail

(*Answers will vary.*)

PART IV PRESENT PERFECT

UNIT PRESENT PERFECT: *SINCE* AND *FOR*

1

2. looked
3. come
4. brought
5. played
6. had
7. gotten
8. fallen
9. watched
10. lost
11. won
12. eaten

2

Since: 4:00 P.M., Monday, yesterday, she was a child
For: a day, an hour, a long time, ten years, many months

3

Biography 1
2. since
3. Since
4. has gone on
5. For
6. have seen
7. Since
8. has earned
9. (has) broken
Biography 2
1. has been
2. for
3. has appeared
4. since
5. Since
6. has received
7. has directed
8. has formed
9. Since
10. has taken on

4

2. A: How long has he been a professional golfer?
   B: (He's been a professional golfer) since he was sixteen. OR for _____ years.
3. A: Has he won any major tournaments since he turned professional?
   B: Yes, he has.
4. A: How long has he been on TV commercials?
   B: (He has been on TV commercials) for the past few years.
5. A: How long has Jodie Foster been an actress?
   B: (She has been an actress) for most of her life.

6. A: Has she won any Oscars since 1985?
B: Yes, she has.
7. A: Has she directed any movies since she graduated from Yale?
B: Yes, she has.
8. A: How long has she been a mother?
B: She has been a mother since (July, 20) 1998 OR for _____ years.

5

3. Min Ho has won three awards
4. Marilyn has appeared in two movies
5. Victor and Marilyn haven't seen each other since 1998.
6. Andreas has lost three games
7. Tanya and Boris have been skaters since 1998.

UNIT **PRESENT PERFECT:**
ALREADY AND YET

1

2. acted	8. danced
3. given	9. fought
4. kept	10. known
5. held	11. drunk
6. traveled	12. smiled
7. sung	

2

1. haven't had, yet
2. 've already gotten, haven't decided yet
3. Have . . . eaten yet, 've already had

3

3. Has she gone food shopping yet? She's already gone food shopping.
4. Has she given the patient medication yet? She's already given the patient medication.
5. Has she called the doctor for the blood-test results yet? She hasn't called the doctor for the blood-test results yet. OR She hasn't yet called the doctor for the blood-test results.
6. Has she changed the patient's bandages yet? She's already changed the patient's bandages.
7. Has she given the patient a bath yet? She hasn't given the patient a bath yet. OR She hasn't yet given the patient a bath.
8. Has she taken the patient's temperature yet? She's already taken the patient's temperature.
9. Has she done the laundry yet? She hasn't done the laundry yet. OR She hasn't yet done the laundry.
10. Has she exercised the patient's legs yet? She hasn't exercised the patient's legs yet. OR She hasn't yet exercised the patient's legs.

4

It's 8:00 p.m. and I'm exhausted. I'm at my new job. I've already ~~work~~ **worked** here for two weeks. The job is hard, but I feel that the patient ~~have~~ **has** already made progress. She hasn't walked ~~already~~ **yet**, but she's already sat up by herself. She can feed herself now, too. ~~Already~~ she has **already** gained three pounds. OR **already**

How are you? When are you coming to visit? Have you ~~decide~~ **decided** yet? Please write.

UNIT **PRESENT PERFECT:**
INDEFINITE PAST

1

2. begun	8. heard
3. forgiven	9. seen
4. promised	10. decided
5. gone	11. kept
6. felt	12. acted
7. grown	

2

2. has acted	6. have . . . felt
3. have seen	7. has kept
4. have begun	8. has promised
5. have heard	

3

2. has chosen
3. have come
4. have been
5. have not been
6. has . . . been
7. has worked
8. have . . . read
9. have rejected
10. have gone
11. have . . . felt
12. have gotten
13. have not
14. have . . . told
15. have played
16. has produced
17. have . . . been
18. have . . . seen

4

2. How many nominations for Best Actor have you received?
3. Have you ever seen your own films?
4. Have you ever gone to the Academy Awards?
5. How many foreign films have you acted in? OR How many times have you acted in foreign films?
6. Have you ever worked with Sophia Loren?
7. Have you (ever) been in a French film?
8. How has it changed your life?
9. Have you read any good scripts lately?

UNIT 19 PRESENT PERFECT AND SIMPLE PAST TENSE

1

2. Joe had
3. Joe got
4. Joe has made
5. Joe has been
6. Joe looked
7. Joe bought
8. Joe has paid
9. Joe has read
10. Joe felt

2

2. got
3. 've been
4. did . . . have
5. became
6. had
7. were
8. did . . . last
9. divorced
10. Did . . . have
11. didn't
12. 've remained
13. saw
14. have become
15. Has . . . remarried
16. hasn't
17. did . . . fail
18. got
19. didn't know
20. did . . . meet
21. were
22. did . . . move
23. 've lived

3

2. began
3. got
4. had
5. was
6. has risen
7. occurred
8. has created
9. began
10. had
11. were
12. has . . . increased
13. stayed
14. got
15. has changed
16. has reached

4

Last month, I have ~~met~~ the most wonderful guy. His name is Roger, and he is a student in my night class. He ~~lived~~ *'s lived* here since 1992. Before that he lived in Detroit too, so we have a lot in

common. Roger ~~has been~~ *was* married for five years but got divorced last April.

Roger and I ~~spent~~ *have spent* a lot of time together. Last week I saw him every night, and this week we've already gotten together three times after class. Monday night we ~~have seen~~ *saw* a great movie. ~~Did you see~~ *Have you seen* The Purple Room? It's playing at all the theaters.

We ~~decided~~ *'ve decided* to take a trip back to Detroit in the summer. Maybe we can get together? It would be great to see you again. Please let me know if you'll be there.

P.S. I'm enclosing a photo of Roger that ~~I've taken~~ *I took* a few weeks ago.

UNIT 20 PRESENT PERFECT PROGRESSIVE

1

2. Amanda has been working at the *Daily News* since 1999 OR for _____ years.
3. She has been writing a series about the homeless for a month OR since last month.
4. The number of homeless Americans has been increasing since 1980 OR for _____ years.
5. Pete has been working at a homeless shelter for a month OR since last month.
6. He has been studying economics for a year OR since last year.
7. Amanda and Pete have been looking for a new apartment for two months.

2

2. hasn't been sleeping
3. hasn't been eating
4. 's been studying
5. hasn't been working
6. 's been raining
7. 's been running
8. hasn't been waiting
9. 've been trying
10. haven't been feeling

3

(Answers will vary.)

2. How long has the police officer been standing
3. How long has the woman been walking
4. How long have the children been playing with the
5. How long has . . . been raining
6. How long have the men been waiting for

UNIT 21 PRESENT PERFECT AND PRESENT PERFECT PROGRESSIVE

1

2. has been selling
3. has been fighting
4. have opened
5. has . . . done
6. has been appearing
7. has been traveling
8. has received
9. has started
10. has written
11. has . . . combined

2

2. have . . . been
3. have . . . been doing
4. 've been reading
5. Have . . . read
6. 've seen
7. Have . . . bought
8. 've been using
9. has . . . opened
10. 've been opening

3

2. How much money has her business made this year?
3. How long has she been traveling around the world?
4. How many countries has she visited?
5. How many copies of her book has she sold?
6. Has she written any books since *Body and Soul*?
7. Has she ever appeared on TV?
8. How long have she and her husband lived in England? OR How long have she and her husband been living in England?

4

It's the second week of the fall semester. I've
been taking
~~taken~~ a business course with Professor McCarthy.
been
For the past two weeks we've ˄ studying people
become
who have ~~been becoming~~ very successful in the
world of business. As part of the course, we've
been reading books by or about internationally

famous businesspeople. For example, I've just
finished
~~been finishing~~ a book by Bill Gates, the CEO of
Microsoft, called <u>Business @ The Speed of</u>
I've been reading
<u>Thought</u>. It was fascinating. Since then ~~I've read~~
<u>Body and Soul</u> by Anita Roddick, the owner of
read
The Body Shop. I've only ~~been reading~~ about fifty
pages of the book so far, but it seems interesting.
've been buying OR 've bought
Although I ~~bought~~ her products ever since one of
her stores opened in my neighborhood, I really
didn't know much about her.

PART V ADJECTIVES AND ADVERBS: REVIEW AND EXPANSION

UNIT 22 ADJECTIVES AND ADVERBS

1

2. nice
3. fast
4. well
5. dangerous
6. beautifully
7. hard
8. safely
9. occasional
10. happy
11. sudden
12. carefully
13. angrily
14. unfortunate

2

2. Good news travels fast!
3. It has five large rooms,
4. it's in a very large building.
5. It's not too bad.
6. It seems pretty quiet.
7. the landlord speaks very loudly.
8. He doesn't hear well.
9. Was it a hard decision?
10. we had to decide quickly.
11. I have to leave now.
12. Good luck with your new apartment!

3

2. hard
3. well
4. nice
5. extremely
6. comfortable
7. cold
8. pretty
9. friendly
10. safe
11. really
12. important
13. late
14. completely
15. empty
16. good
17. easily
18. near
19. frequently
20. wonderful

4

2. disturbed
3. entertaining
4. disgusted
5. inspiring
6. paralyzed
7. moving
8. moved
9. frightening
10. disturbed
11. touching
12. astonishing
13. frightening
14. bored
15. disappointed
16. touching
17. exciting
18. entertaining
19. bored

UNIT **ADJECTIVES: COMPARATIVES AND EQUATIVES**

1

2. more expensive
3. hotter
4. bigger
5. better
6. more difficult
7. prettier
8. more beautiful
9. worse
10. longer
11. farther
12. more careful
13. more dangerous
14. earlier
15. more terrible
16. wider
17. noisier
18. more comfortable
19. wetter
20. cheaper

2

2. larger
3. slower
4. bigger than
5. more quiet / quieter
6. more expensive
7. cheaper than
8. better
9. more convenient
10. farther
11. faster than
12. more comfortable
13. later than
14. settled

3

2. Y . . . cheaper than . . . X.
3. Y . . . larger than . . . X.
4. Y . . . heavier than . . . X.
5. X . . . more efficient than . . . Y.
6. Y . . . more effective than . . . X.
7. Y . . . faster than . . . X.
8. X . . . noisier than . . . Y.
9. Y . . . better than . . . X.
10. X . . . worse than . . . Y.

4

2. not as crowded as
3. not as big as
4. not as cold as
5. as hot as
6. not as wet as
7. not as windy as
8. not as sunny as

5

2. The smaller the city, the lower the crime rate.
3. The warmer the climate, the busier the police.
4. The colder the weather, the greater the number of robberies.
5. The larger the police force, the more violent the city.
6. The later in the day, the higher the number of car thefts.
7. The higher the unemployment rate, the higher the crime rate.
8. The more mobile the population, the more dangerous the city.
9. The more organized the community, the safer the neighborhood.

6

2. is getting less and less crowded.
3. is getting lower and lower.
4. is getting higher and higher.
5. are getting more and more expensive.

7

(Answers will vary.)

UNIT **ADJECTIVES: SUPERLATIVES**

1

2. the funniest
3. the biggest
4. the most wonderful
5. the best
6. the worst
7. the happiest
8. the most important
9. the warmest
10. the most interesting
11. the farthest
12. the most intelligent
13. the slowest
14. the most expensive

2

2. The least expensive
3. Funji
4. the most expensive
5. Minon
6. the lowest
7. Minon
8. the smallest
9. the lightest
10. the most powerful
11. the heaviest
12. Minon
13. the most convenient
14. Rikon
15. the least important

3

2. the smallest
3. the deepest
4. the tallest
5. the longest
6. the farthest
7. the busiest
8. the most popular
9. the most expensive
10. the fastest
11. the slowest
12. the heaviest

UNIT ADVERBS: EQUATIVES, COMPARATIVES, SUPERLATIVES

1

2. faster   the fastest
3. more beautifully   the most beautifully
4. sooner   the soonest
5. more dangerously   the most dangerously
6. better   the best
7. earlier   the earliest
8. more carefully   the most carefully
9. worse   the worst
10. farther   the farthest

2

2. harder than
3. more slowly than OR slower than
4. faster
5. more accurately
6. more aggressively than
7. worse than
8. better
9. more successfully
10. more seriously
11. more regularly than

Winning Team Members: George, Bob, Randy, Dennis
Losing Team Members: Alex, Rick, Larry, Elvin

3

2. ran as fast as
3. jumped as high as
4. didn't jump as high as
5. didn't throw the discus as far as
6. threw the discus as far as
7. didn't do as well as
8. didn't compete as successfully as

4

2. E . . . the slowest OR the most slowly . . . slower OR more slowly than
3. higher than . . . B
4. E . . . the highest
5. farther than . . . E
6. E . . . the farthest
7. E . . . the best

5

2. She's running more and more frequently.
3. He's throwing the ball farther and farther.
4. She's shooting more and more accurately.
5. He's jumping higher and higher.
6. He's running slower and slower OR more and more slowly.
7. They're skating more and more gracefully.

8. They're practicing harder and harder.
9. He's driving more and more dangerously.

6

I just completed my run. I'm running much
    than
longer ~~that~~ before. Today I ran for thirty minutes
without getting out of breath. I'm glad I decided
    more slowly OR slower
to run ~~more slow~~. The more slowly I run, the
farther
~~farthest~~ I can go. I'm really seeing progress.
Because I'm enjoying it, I run more and more
frequently
~~frequent~~. And the more often I do it, the longer
and farther I can go. I really believe that running
     quickly
lets me feel better more ~~quick~~ than other forms of
exercise. I'm even sleeping better than before!

I'm thinking about running in the next
   as fast as OR faster than
marathon. I may not run ~~as fast than~~ younger
     longer
runners, but I think I can run ~~long~~ and farther.
We'll see!

PART VI GERUNDS AND INFINITIVES

UNIT 26 GERUNDS: SUBJECT AND OBJECT

1

2. going   7. doing
3. meeting   8. taking
4. Sitting   9. Exercising
5. running   10. wasting
6. lifting

2

2. lifting weights
3. playing tennis
4. dancing
5. Doing sit-ups
6. lifting weights
7. Dancing
8. Walking
9. dancing
10. jogging
11. doing sit-ups OR playing tennis OR jogging
12. doing sit-ups OR playing tennis OR jogging

3

2. dislikes doing
3. enjoys dancing
4. mind teaching
5. kept practicing
6. denied OR denies stepping

7. considering taking
8. regrets not beginning
9. suggests going
10. admits feeling

(Answers will vary.)

UNIT 27 GERUNDS AFTER PREPOSITIONS

2. of   **7.** of
3. to   **8.** in
4. on   **9.** about
5. in   **10.** to
6. for OR to

2

2. succeeded in collecting
3. is worried about missing
4. are used to working
5. believe in talking
6. are tired of waiting
7. insists on reaching
8. approves of having
9. are opposed to going
10. looking forward to returning

3

2. striking   **7.** missing
3. firing   **8.** trying
4. permitting   **9.** making
5. being   **10.** hearing
6. getting

4

(Answers will vary.)

UNIT 28 INFINITIVES AFTER CERTAIN VERBS

2. want to see
3. refuses to go
4. threatened to end
5. hesitate OR am hesitating to take
6. seems to be
7. attempted to create
8. intend to stay

9. needs to speak
10. will agree to go

2. to do the dishes, him to do the dishes.
3. her to buy some milk, to buy some milk.
4. him to drive her to her aunt's, to drive her to her aunt's.
5. him to have dinner at her place, to have dinner at her place.
6. him to give her his answer, to give her his answer.
7. to cut his hair, her to cut his hair.
8. him to be home at 7:00, to be home at 8:00.
9. her to call him before she leaves the office, to call him before she left the office.

Gabby answered my letter! She advised ~~we~~ **us** to go to counseling separately. I don't know if John will agree ~~going~~ **to go**, but I'm going to ask him to think about it. I attempted to introduce the topic last night, but he pretended ~~to~~ **not to** ~~not~~ hear me. I won't give up, though. I'm going to try to persuade him to go. Our relationship deserves to have a chance, and I'm prepared **to** give it onc. But I want John ~~feels~~ **to feel** the same way. I'm patient, but I can't afford ~~waiting~~ **to wait** forever.

(Answers will vary.)

UNIT 29 INFINITIVES OF PURPOSE

3. She used her credit card in order not to pay right away.
4. I asked for the dressing room (in order) to try on a dress.
5. They went to the snack bar (in order) to get a drink.
6. I'm going to wait for a sale (in order) to save some money.
7. She tried on the blouse (in order) to be sure of the size.
8. He only took fifty dollars with him in order not to spend more.

9. They went to Lacy's on Monday in order not to miss the sale.
10. I always go shopping early (in order) to avoid the crowds.

2

2. (in order) to return
3. in order not to pay
4. (in order) to carry
5. (in order) to sign
6. to have

7. (in order) to cut
8. (in order) to find out
9. in order not to miss
10. in order not to waste

3

I went to the store ~~for~~ to get some eggs and other things for dinner. I set the alarm on the electronic organizer to remind you to put the turkey in the oven. Could you call Cindi ~~too~~ ^{to} ask her to bring some dessert? Tell her she should come straight from school in order ^{not to be} ~~to be not~~ late. We'll eat at 6:00—if that's OK with you. Remember—you can use the Datalator ^{to check} ~~for checking~~ the vegetable casserole recipe. I've got to run in order to get back in time to help you!

UNIT 30 INFINITIVES WITH *TOO* AND *ENOUGH*

1

2. It's too noisy for me to concentrate.
3. The work is varied enough to be interesting.
4. The salary is high enough for me to support my family.
5. My desk is too small to hold all my things.
6. I can sleep late enough to feel awake in the morning.
7. My boss speaks too quickly for me to understand him.
8. The bookshelves aren't low enough for me to reach.

Positive points: 1,3,4,6,9
Negative points: 2,5,7,8,10

2

2. late enough to call
3. too heavy for me to carry
4. too sweet to drink

5. small enough to fit
6. too noisy for me to think
7. not old enough to retire
8. not hot enough to need
9. not sick enough to call
10. too high for me to reach

3

I'm almost ^{too} ~~to~~ tired to write. I can't believe how hard Boy Scout camp is. Today we went out on a two-hour hike. It was over 90° in the shade! It was too hot ^{to think OR for me to think} ~~for to think~~. We had to take a lot of stuff with us, too. My backpack was too heavy for me to lift ~~it~~. I don't think I'm ^{strong enough} ~~too strong~~ to complete the program. How did I get into this mess? Is it too late ^{to} ~~too~~ get out? Please write.

P.S. The food is terrible. It's not ^{good enough} ~~enough good~~ to eat. Can you send some candy bars?

P.P.S. Here's a photo of me in case it's been ^{too} ~~too~~ long for you to remember what I look like!

4

(Answers will vary.)

UNIT 31 GERUNDS AND INFINITIVES

1

3. to leave
4. walking
5. to be
6. to look

7. taking
8. to ask
9. living
10. seeing

2

2. is tired of being
3. quit drinking
4. believes in working
5. forgot to bring
6. remember locking
7. stopped to get

8. afford to move
9. refuses to live
10. intends to get
11. agreed to help
12. offered to drive

3

3. Being cautious is wise.
4. It's dangerous to walk on ice.
5. It's a good idea to install a burglar alarm.

6. Being afraid all the time isn't good.
7. It's risky to walk alone on a dark, deserted street.
8. It's helpful to work together.

(Answers will vary.)

PART VII MORE MODALS AND RELATED VERBS AND EXPRESSIONS

UNIT **PREFERENCES:**
PREFER, WOULD PREFER,
WOULD RATHER

2. listen to music than go for a walk.
3. reading a book to visiting friends.
4. visiting friends to talking on the phone.
5. go to the movies than watch TV.
6. talk on the phone than listen to music.
7. going to the movies to playing cards.
8. watching TV to listening to music.
9. read a book than watch TV.
10. reading a book to playing cards.

2

2. He'd prefer (to have) juice.
3. He'd rather have tomato juice than apple juice.
4. He'd rather not have a hot beverage.
5. He'd prefer not to have chicken soup.
6. He'd prefer a sandwich to cottage cheese and fruit.
7. He'd prefer a turkey sandwich to a tuna fish sandwich.
8. He'd rather have white bread.
9. He'd rather not have chocolate pudding.
10. He'd prefer vanilla ice cream to chocolate ice cream.

3

2. Do you prefer
3. Would you rather
4. would you rather
5. Would you rather
6. Would you prefer
7. Would you prefer
8. Do you prefer

(Answers will vary.)

UNIT **NECESSITY:**
HAVE (GOT) TO, DON'T HAVE TO,
MUST, MUST NOT, CAN'T,

1

2. must not allow
3. must be
4. must send
5. must not drive
6. must place
7. must turn on
8. must not wear
9. must stop
10. must not drink

2

2. don't have to be
3. don't have to take
4. have to complete
5. don't have to renew
6. have to renew
7. have to pay
8. don't have to pay
9. have to take
10. don't have to get
11. have to wear
12. don't have to wear

3

2. don't have to
3. don't have to
4. don't have to
5. must not
6. don't have to
7. don't have to
8. must not
9. must not
10. don't have to

4

2. **A:** Do . . . have to stop
   B: Yes, we do
3. **A:** have . . . had to use
4. **A:** Did . . . have to work
   B: No, I didn't
5. **B:** 'll have to get OR 'm going to have to get
6. **B:** had to drive
7. **B:** did . . . have to pay
8. **A:** Has . . . had to pay
   B: No, he hasn't
9. **A:** Will OR Do . . . have to get OR Are . . . going to have to get
   B: Yes, I will OR do OR am
10. **B:** has to have

5

2. b.
3. b.
4. c.
5. a.
6. b.
7. a.
8. b.

6

(Answers will vary.)

UNIT EXPECTATIONS:
BE SUPPOSED TO

❶

2. is supposed to send
3. are supposed to provide
4. isn't supposed to pay for
5. is supposed to pay for
6. aren't supposed to finance
7. is supposed to finance
8. aren't supposed to give
9. isn't supposed to supply
10. is supposed to pay for

❷

2. Item 2. She was supposed to write the month first. OR She wasn't supposed to write the day first.
3. Item 4. She was supposed to print OR write her last name. OR She wasn't supposed to print OR write her first name.
4. Item 5. She was supposed to print OR write her first name. OR She wasn't supposed to print OR write her last name.
5. Item 6. She was supposed to write OR include her zip code.
6. Item 7. She was supposed to write her state.
7. Item 8. She was supposed to sign her name. OR She wasn't supposed to print her name.
8. Item 9. She was supposed to write the date.

❸

1. F: is OR was supposed to land
2. L: are . . . supposed to get
3. L: Are . . . supposed to call; F: Yes, we are
4. F: are . . . supposed to tip
5. F: Is . . . supposed to be; F: No, it isn't
6. L: are . . . supposed to do; F: 're supposed to leave
7. L: Is . . . supposed to rain; F: No, it isn't
8. F: Are . . . supposed to shake

UNIT FUTURE POSSIBILITY:
MAY, MIGHT, COULD

❶

2. may go
3. could be
4. might want
5. may not be
6. might not be
7. could go
8. might not understand
9. might not want to
10. could stay

❷

2. might buy
3. is going to rain
4. is going to see
5. might go
6. is going to work
7. might have
8. is going to call
9. is going to read
10. might write

❸

How are you? It's the Fourth of July, and it's raining really hard. They say it could clear up later. Then again, it ~~could~~ not. You never know with the weather. *(might OR may above "could")*

Do you remember my brother, Ed? He says hi. He might ~~has~~ dinner with me on Saturday night. We may go to a new Mexican restaurant that opened in the mall. *(have above "has")*

I definitely ~~might take~~ some vacation next month. Perhaps we could do something together. It might ~~not~~ be fun to do some traveling. What do you think? Let me know. *(am going to take OR am taking above "might take")*

❹

(Answers will vary.)

UNIT ASSUMPTIONS:
MUST, HAVE (GOT) TO, MAY,
MIGHT, COULD, CAN'T

❶

2. must not be
3. must feel
4. must not have
5. must know
6. must have
7. must not hear
8. must feel
9. must speak
10. must not study
11. must have
12. must not eat

❷

2. might
3. must
4. must
5. might
6. could
7. could
8. must
9. must
10. couldn't

3

2. She must
3. They must
4. He must be
5. She might
6. It must be

7. They might be
8. She must
9. He might be
10. They must be

4

2. Could
3. can't
4. Bob
5. Chet
6. could

7. might
8. Dave
9. could
10. couldn't
11. Allen

5

(Answers will vary)

6

Just got home. It's really cold outside. The
temperature ~~could~~ **must** be below freezing because the
walkway is all covered with ice. What a day! We
went down to the police station to look at photos.
They must ~~having~~ **have** hundreds of photos. They kept
showing us more and more. We kept looking, but
it was difficult to be sure. After all, we only saw
the burglar for a few seconds. They've ~~gotta~~ **got to** have
other witnesses besides us! There were a lot of
people at the mall that day. We ~~may not~~ **can't OR couldn't** be the
only ones who got a look at the burglar! That's
the one thing I'm certain of! In spite of our
uncertainty with the photos, the detective was
very patient. I guess he must be used to
witnesses like us. Nevertheless, it ~~have~~ **has** to be
frustrating for him. I know the police ~~may~~ **must** really
want to catch this guy.

PART VIII NOUNS AND ARTICLES

UNIT 37 NOUNS AND QUANTIFIERS

1

Proper nouns: Election Day, Japanese, Richard,
Yeltsin
Common count nouns: chair, class, country, day,
dollar, hamburger, pen, president, snowflake,
story, zoo

Common non-count nouns: biology, furniture,
honesty, ink, money, news, rice, snow, spaghetti,
sugar, swimming

2

2. Potatoes are . . . Rice is
3. Potato chips are
4. Americans eat . . . people
5. kills
6. Popcorn is
7. Peanuts are not
8. Peanut butter has
9. history . . . is
10. Ice cream is

3

2. many (c.)
3. much (b.)
4. many (c.)
5. much (b.)

6. many (b.)
7. much (b.)
8. many (a.)

4

2. many
3. few
4. many
5. much
6. Several

7. some
8. a few
9. much
10. enough

5

(Answers will vary.)

UNIT 38 ARTICLES: INDEFINITE AND DEFINITE

1

1. the . . . the
2. the
3. the
4. the . . . the
5. a . . . The . . . the
6. the
7. Ø . . . Ø
8. the . . . a
9. an . . . a
10. Ø . . . Ø
11. some . . . a . . . the . . . the
12. the . . . a . . . The

2

2. a	13. the
3. A	14. the
4. a	15. the
5. Ø	16. the
6. Ø	17. the
7. a	18. an
8. Ø	19. Ø
9. The	20. a
10. Ø	21. Ø
11. a	22. the
12. The	

3

2. a	15. an
3. a	16. the
4. the	17. the
5. the	18. The
6. the	19. a
7. the	20. the
8. the	21. the
9. the	22. the
10. The	23. The
11. the	24. the
12. a	25. the
13. the	26. Ø
14. the	27. the

Test: Units 1–8

DIRECTIONS: *Circle the letter of the correct answer to complete each sentence.*

Example:

Jackie never _____ coffee. A **(B)** C D

    (A) drink   (C) is drinking
    (B) drinks   (D) was drinking

1. At the moment, Meng _____ on a report.   A B C D
    (A) doesn't work   (C) work
    (B) is working   (D) works

2. Water _____ at 100°C.   A B C D
    (A) boil   (C) boils
    (B) boiling   (D) is boiling

3. What _____ these days?   A B C D
    (A) are you doing   (C) you are doing
    (B) do you do   (D) you do

4. Do you have any aspirin? George _____ a headache.   A B C D
    (A) are having   (C) have
    (B) has   (D) is having

5. Alicia _____ to the park every day.   A B C D
    (A) does   (C) goes
    (B) go   (D) is going

6. When you get to the corner, _____ left.   A B C D
    (A) is turning   (C) turning
    (B) turn   (D) turns

7. Walk! _____ run!   A B C D
    (A) Don't   (C) Not
    (B) No   (D) You don't

8. Jennifer never _____ in the ocean.   A B C D
   (A) is swimming   (C) swimming
   (B) swim   (D) swims

9. A: Do you like spaghetti?   A B C D
   B: Yes, I _____.
   (A) am   (C) don't
   (B) do   (D) like

10. Roger _____ me at 9:00 last night.   A B C D
    (A) called   (C) is calling
    (B) calls   (D) was calling

11. There _____ a lot of people in the park yesterday.   A B C D
    (A) are   (C) was
    (B) is   (D) were

12. One day last March, I _____ a very strange letter.   A B C D
    (A) did get   (C) used to get
    (B) got   (D) was getting

13. Where _____ to school?   A B C D
    (A) did you go   (C) you go
    (B) you did go   (D) you went

14. Claude didn't _____ in Canada.   A B C D
    (A) lived   (C) used to live
    (B) use to live   (D) used to living

15. Rick left class early because he _____ a headache.   A B C D
    (A) had   (C) used to have
    (B) have   (D) was having

16. _____ is your English teacher?   A B C D
    (A) Who   (C) Whose
    (B) Whom   (D) Why

17. Who _____ yesterday at the store?   A B C D
    (A) did you see   (C) you saw
    (B) did you use to see   (D) you were seeing

18. As soon as the light turned red, she _____ the car. A B C D
    (A) did stop   (C) stops
    (B) stopped   (D) was stopping

19. They _____ when the phone rang.   A B C D
    (A) sleep   (C) was sleeping
    (B) slept   (D) were sleeping

20. Johnny _____ the paper when I interrupted him.   A   B   C   D

(A) read   (C) was reading
(B) reads   (D) were reading

21. **A:** Who _____ there?   A   B   C   D
B: Mr. Jackson saw me.

(A) did you see   (C) you saw
(B) saw you   (D) you see

22. **A:** Whose teacher _____?   A   B   C   D
B: I called Jack's teacher.

(A) called you   (C) you called
(B) did you call   (D) were calling

23. It _____ tomorrow.   A   B   C   D

(A) rains   (C) 's going to rain
(B) rained   (D) 's raining

24. Don't eat so much. You _____ sick later.   A   B   C   D

(A) 're feeling   (C) felt
(B) feel   (D) 'll feel

25. The package will _____ tomorrow.   A   B   C   D

(A) arrive   (C) arriving
(B) arrives   (D) be going to arrive

26. What _____ you do next month when you finish this   A   B   C   D
course?

(A) are   (C) do
(B) did   (D) will

27. Goodnight. I _____ tomorrow.   A   B   C   D

(A) 'll see you   (C) 'm seeing you
(B) 'm going to see you   (D) see

28. Mike and I _____ to the Crash concert. We already have   A   B   C   D
our tickets.

(A) are going   (C) went
(B) go   (D) will go

29. What will Michiko do when she _____ her license?   A   B   C   D

(A) gets   (C) is going to get
(B) is getting   (D) will get

30. That driver _____ a speeding ticket. The police are right A   B   C   D
behind him.

(A) gets   (C) is going to get
(B) is getting   (D) will get

31. The car of the future _____ on electricity.   A B C D
  (A) is running   (C) runs
  (B) ran   (D) will run

32. According to this schedule, the next train _____ in ten   A B C D
  minutes.
  (A) leave   (C) left
  (B) leaves   (D) leaving

33. **A:** Will you be home tomorrow night?   A B C D
  B: No, _____.
  (A) I don't   (C) I will
  (B) I'm not   (D) I won't

34. I'll see you _____.   A B C D
  (A) at the moment   (C) last night
  (B) in an hour   (D) usually

35. **A:** Why did you borrow those chairs from Jimmy?   A B C D
  B: I _____ a party next Saturday night.
  (A) had   (C) 'm going to have
  (B) have   (D) 'll have

36. **A:** Call me when you get home.   A B C D
  B: Don't worry. I _____.
  (A) don't forget   (C) 'm not forgetting
  (B) forget   (D) won't forget

PART TWO

DIRECTIONS: Each sentence has four underlined words or phrases. The four underlined parts of the sentence are marked A, B, C, and D. Circle the letter of the <u>one</u> underlined word or phrase that is NOT CORRECT.

Example:

Ana <u>rarely is drinking</u> coffee, but <u>this morning</u> she <u>is having</u> a cup.   A (B) C D
　　 A　　　　 B　　　　　　　　 C　　　　　 D

37. Terry <u>usually</u> <u>drives</u> to work, but <u>today</u> she <u>takes</u> the train.   A B C D
　　　　 A　　　 B　　　　　 C　　　 D

38. Carlos <u>usually</u> doesn't <u>eat</u> pizza, but <u>at</u> the moment he   A B C D
　　　　　 A　　　　　 B　　　　 C
  <u>is wanting</u> a slice.
　　 D

39. Frank <u>rarely</u> <u>goes</u> downtown because he <u>doesn't</u> <u>likes</u> the   A B C D
　　　　 A　　 B　　　　　　　　　　 C　　 D
  crowded streets.

40. Ana <u>usually</u> <u>is eating</u> in the cafeteria, but <u>these days</u> she <u>is eating</u> **A B C D**
        A   B   C   D
in the park.

41. <u>What</u> <u>you are</u> <u>studying</u> these days <u>at school</u>? **A B C D**
     A   B   C   D

42. Jackie <u>don't</u> <u>speak</u> French, but <u>she's</u> <u>studying</u> Spanish at the **A B C D**
            A   B   C   D
Adult Center.

43. Julie <u>loves</u> tennis, but <u>rarely she</u> <u>plays</u> because she <u>doesn't have</u> time. **A B C D**
        A   B   C   D

44. <u>Stand</u> up straight, <u>breathe</u> deeply, <u>hold</u> your head up, and <u>no look</u> **A B C D**
     A   B   C   D
down.

45. John <u>works always</u> late and <u>is</u> <u>rarely</u> home before 8:00 <u>at night</u>. **A B C D**
        A   B C   D

46. I <u>know</u> you usually <u>don't wear</u> a jacket, but <u>wear</u> one today because **A B C D**
    A   B   C
it <u>is feeling</u> cold outside.
    D

47. A breeze <u>is blowing</u>, the <u>sun</u> <u>shines</u>, and the sky <u>looks</u> clear and **A B C D**
           A   B C   D
bright.

48. Paul <u>was</u> <u>drying</u> the dishes <u>when</u> he <u>was dropping</u> the plate. **A B C D**
       A   B   C   D

49. When Gloria <u>were</u> a little girl, she <u>used to</u> <u>pretend</u> that she <u>had</u> a **A B C D**
             A   B   C   D
horse.

50. What <u>did</u> you <u>used to</u> <u>do</u> when you <u>felt</u> afraid? **A B C D**
       A   B C   D

51. <u>As soon as</u> the alarm clock <u>rang</u>, she <u>woke up</u> and <u>was getting</u> out **A B C D**
     A   B   C   D
of bed.

52. Once <u>when</u> I <u>was</u> a little boy, I <u>used to get</u> sick and <u>went</u> to the **A B C D**
        A   B   C   D
hospital.

53. Who <u>you did</u> <u>see</u> when you <u>left</u> the building <u>last night</u>? **A B C D**
        A   B   C   D

54. <u>While</u> I <u>drove</u> home, I <u>turned on</u> the car radio and <u>heard</u> the news **A B C D**
     A   B   C   D
about the accident.

55. When Marie <u>will get</u> <u>home</u>, she <u>is going to</u> <u>call</u> me. **A B C D**
            A   B   C   D

56. <u>As soon as</u> she <u>finds</u> a new <u>job</u>, she <u>tells</u> her boss.   **A B C D**
        A   B   C   D

57. <u>I'll make</u> some sandwiches <u>before</u> <u>I'll leave</u> for the office   **A B C D**
     A   B   C

 <u>in the morning</u>.
     D

58. According to the weather <u>forecast</u>, it <u>going to be</u> hot and sunny   **A B C D**
                             A   B

 <u>tomorrow</u> with a chance of a thunderstorm <u>in the afternoon</u>.
    C   D

59. The doors <u>will</u> open until the train <u>comes</u> to a <u>complete</u> <u>stop</u>.   **A B C D**
            A   B   C   D

60. My sister <u>is going to be</u> sixteen <u>next</u> month, and she <u>has</u> a big party   **A B C D**
             A   B   C   D

 with all her friends.

TEST: UNITS 9–10

DIRECTIONS: *Circle the letter of the correct answer to complete each sentence.*

Example:

Jackie never _____ coffee.　　　　A **Ⓑ** C D

   (A) drink　　　　　　　　(C) is drinking
   (B) drinks　　　　　　　　(D) was drinking

1. Karen lives by _____ but she's looking　　A B C D
   for a roomate.
   (A) her　　　　　　　　　(C) himself
   (B) herself　　　　　　　(D) ourselves

2. People in my office exchange cards with　　A B C D
   _____ during the holidays.
   (A) myself　　　　　　　(C) ourselves
   (B) one another　　　　　(D) themselves

3. Thanks for offering to help, but I think I can do　　A B C D
   it _____.
   (A) herself　　　　　　　(C) itself
   (B) himself　　　　　　　(D) myself

4. **A:** Sara is talking to Pete.　　A B C D
   B: I didn't know that they knew _____.
   (A) each other　　　　　(C) them
   (B) others　　　　　　　(D) themselves

5. **A:** Did you say something to me?　　A B C D
   B: No, I'm just talking to _____. I do
   that sometimes when I'm cooking.
   (A) me　　　　　　　　　(C) oneself
   (B) myself　　　　　　　(D) you

6. **A:** Help _____.
   B: Thanks.
   (A) me   (C) you
   (B) myself   (D) yourself

   A   B   C   D

7. **A:** Where are your books?
   B: I put _____ .
   (A) away   (C) them away
   (B) away them   (D) them off

   A   B   C   D

8. It's an interesting story. Please _____.
   (A) carry out   (C) hand in
   (B) go on   (D) write up

   A   B   C   D

9. When Mei-Ling doesn't know a word, she always looks it
   _____ in the dictionary.
   (A) at   (C) over
   (B) into   (D) up

   A   B   C   D

10. Please call _____ up when you get home.
    (A) me   (C) you
    (B) myself   (D) yourself

    A   B   C   D

11. It's my own fault. That's why I'm angry at _____.
    (A) him   (C) me
    (B) himself   (D) myself

    A   B   C   D

PART TWO

DIRECTIONS: Each sentence has four underlined words or phrases. The four underlined parts of the sentence are marked A, B, C, and D. Circle the letter of the <u>one</u> underlined word or phrase that is NOT CORRECT.

Example:

Ana <u>rarely</u> <u>is drinking</u> coffee, but <u>this morning</u> she <u>is having</u> a cup.
     A   B   C   D

A (B) C   D

12. Could we talk <u>over it</u> before you <u>turn</u> the whole <u>idea</u> <u>down</u>?
                 A   B   C   D

    A   B   C   D

13. Jake <u>stood</u> <u>up</u> and introduced <u>himself</u> to <u>myself</u>.
        A   B   C   D

    A   B   C   D

14. Marta <u>herself</u> <u>call</u> the meeting <u>off</u> <u>yesterday</u>.
          A   B   C   D

    A   B   C   D

15. Do you want to get up <u>by</u> <u>yourself</u>, or would you like me to
                   A   B

    <u>wake</u> <u>up you</u>?
      C   D

    A   B   C   D

16. Don't <u>clean</u> <u>up</u> the kitchen by <u>itself</u>; I'd be glad to <u>help out</u>.
           A   B   C   D

    A   B   C   D

17. Rachel and Rick know <u>themselves</u> well because <u>they</u> <u>grew</u> <u>up</u> together.   **A**   **B**   **C**   **D**
                            A   B   C   D

18. Sal and Christel always <u>look over</u> <u>each other</u> homework before they   **A**   **B**   **C**   **D**
                                  A   B

<u>hand</u> <u>it in</u>.
 C   D

19. Before they <u>turned</u> <u>the music</u> <u>down</u>, I couldn't hear <u>me</u> think!   **A**   **B**   **C**   **D**
                     A   B   C   D

20. Tom asked <u>me</u> to <u>pick</u> some stamps for <u>him</u> at the post office <u>up</u>.   **A**   **B**   **C**   **D**
                  A   B   C   D

Test: Units 11–15

Part One

DIRECTIONS: Circle the letter of the correct answer to complete each sentence.

Example:

Jackie never _____ coffee. **A (B) C D**

   (A) drink   (C) is drinking

   (B) drinks   (D) was drinking

1. **A:** Would you shut the door please?   **A B C D**
   B: _____
   (A) Certainly.   (C) Yes, I could.
   (B) No, I can't.   (D) Yes, I would.

2. Why _____ a movie tonight?   **A B C D**
   (A) about seeing   (C) not seeing
   (B) don't we see   (D) we don't see

3. Marcia can't speak German yet, but after a few   **A B C D**
   lessons she _____ speak a little.
   (A) can   (C) is able to
   (B) could   (D) will be able to

4. In 1998, Tara Lipinski _____ win the   **A B C D**
   gold medal in figure skating at the Winter
   Olympics.
   (A) can   (C) will be able to
   (B) could   (D) was able to

5. I _____ make new friends since I   **A B C D**
   moved here.
   (A) can't   (C) haven't been able to
   (B) couldn't   (D) 'm not able to

6. She _____ better not arrive late.   A B C D
    (A) did   (C) had
    (B) has   (D) would

7. A: Do you mind if I borrow a chair?   A B C D
    B: _____ Do you only need one?
    (A) I'm sorry.   (C) Yes, I do.
    (B) Not at all.   (D) Yes, I would.

8. Would you mind _____ me tomorrow?   A B C D
    (A) call   (C) to call
    (B) calling   (D) if you call

9. You _____ miss the deadline or you'll have to pay a late fee.   A B C D
    (A) better not   (C) 'd better not
    (B) 'd better   (D) had no better

10. _____ take the train instead of the bus? It's faster.   A B C D
    (A) How about   (C) Why don't
    (B) Let's   (D) Why not

11. May my sister _____ to class with me tomorrow?   A B C D
    (A) come   (C) coming
    (B) comes   (D) to come

12. A: Would you please explain that again?   A B C D
    B: Yes, _____.
    (A) certainly   (C) Not at all
    (B) I would   (D) I do

PART TWO

DIRECTIONS: Each sentence has four underlined words or phrases. The four underlined parts of the sentence are marked A, B, C, and D. Circle the letter of the <u>one</u> underlined word or phrase that is NOT CORRECT.

Example:

Ana <u>rarely</u> <u>is drinking</u> coffee, but <u>this morning</u> she <u>is having</u> a cup.   A ⒝ C D
    A   B   C   D

13. When <u>you will</u> <u>be</u> <u>able to</u> <u>tell</u> me your decision?   A B C D
            A   B   C   D

14. <u>Why don't</u> <u>we</u> <u>see</u> a movie Friday night<u>.</u>   A B C D
       A   B   C   D

15. <u>Do</u> you <u>mind</u> <u>when</u> I postpone our Wednesday appointment<u>?</u>   A B C D
    A   B   C   D

16. <u>May</u> <u>he</u> <u>has</u> until <u>tomorrow</u> to hand in his paper?   A B C D
    A B C   D

17. <u>Let's</u> <u>to leave</u> the party <u>early enough</u> <u>to catch</u> the last bus.   **A B C D**
   A B   C   D

18. <u>Could</u> you <u>remember</u> <u>to bring</u> home <u>please</u> the newspaper?   **A B C D**
   A   B   C   D

19. You really ought <u>be</u> <u>more</u> <u>careful</u> or you <u>'ll get</u> into trouble.   **A B C D**
        A B   C   D

20. <u>Would</u> you mind <u>to tell</u> me when you <u>are going to</u> <u>be</u> late?   **A B C D**
   A   B   C   D

TEST: UNITS 16–21

T13

PART ONE

DIRECTIONS: Circle the letter of the correct answer to complete each sentence.

Example:

Jackie never _____ coffee.　　　　　A (B) C D

    (A) drink　　　　　　　　　(C) is drinking

    (B) drinks　　　　　　　　　(D) was drinking

1. Anita _____ in Texas since 1991.　　　A B C D

    (A) is living　　　　　　　　(C) have lived

    (B) has lived　　　　　　　　(D) lived

2. John has already _____ this course.　　A B C D

    (A) been taking　　　　　　　(C) takes

    (B) taken　　　　　　　　　(D) took

3. The journalist hasn't finished the article　　　A B C D

   _____.

    (A) already　　　　　　　　(C) then

    (B) now　　　　　　　　　　(D) yet

4. The department store has been in business　　A B C D

   _____ many years.

    (A) already　　　　　　　　(C) in

    (B) for　　　　　　　　　　(D) since

5. How many cups of coffee have you　　　　　A B C D

   _____ this morning?

    (A) been drinking　　　　　　(C) drink

    (B) drank　　　　　　　　　(D) drunk

6. Sheila _____ New Mexico six years ago.　A B C D

    (A) has been leaving　　　　　(C) left

    (B) has left　　　　　　　　(D) used to leave

7. They have been _____ lunch in the same cafeteria for ten years.

    (A) ate   (C) eaten

    (B) eat   (D) eating

                                   A   B   C   D

8. The Jordans _____ at R & J Corp. since 1992.

    (A) are working   (C) have been working

    (B) has been working   (D) worked

                                   A   B   C   D

9. Have you read any good books _____?

    (A) already   (C) lately

    (B) ever   (D) now

                                   A   B   C   D

10. It's _____ all day.

    (A) is raining   (C) has rained

    (B) has been raining   (D) rained

                                   A   B   C   D

11. **A:** Has the mail come yet?

    B: Yes, it _____.

    (A) did   (C) have

    (B) has   (D) is

                                   A   B   C   D

12. I'm sorry I'm late. How long _____?

    (A) did you wait   (C) have you waited

    (B) have you been waiting (D) you have been waiting

                                   A   B   C   D

13. **A:** What are you doing?

    B: I _____ on this report all morning.

    (A) 'm working   (C) 've worked

    (B) 've been working   (D) worked

                                   A   B   C   D

14. _____ you cut your hair lately?

    (A) Are   (C) Has

    (B) Did   (D) Have

                                   A   B   C   D

PART TWO

DIRECTIONS: Each sentence has four underlined words or phrases. The four underlined parts of the sentence are marked A, B, C, and D. Circle the letter of the <u>one</u> underlined word or phrase that is NOT CORRECT.

Example:

Ana <u>rarely</u> <u>is drinking</u> coffee, but <u>this morning</u> she <u>is having</u> a cup.
     A   B   C   D

                                 A (B) C   D

15. <u>When</u> she <u>was</u> a child, she <u>has worked</u> in a factory <u>for</u> more than
    A   B   C   D

    three years.

                                   A   B   C   D

16. Erik <u>have</u> <u>been sleeping</u> <u>for</u> more than <u>three hours</u>.   **A B C D**
        A   B   C   D

17. Last night we <u>have rented</u> two <u>videos</u> and <u>watched</u> them with some   **A B C D**
                     A   B   C

    <u>friends</u>.
    D

18. Jack <u>hasn't</u> <u>done</u> a thing <u>since</u> he <u>has gotten</u> to work.   **A B C D**
          A   B   C   D

19. <u>Since</u> I <u>have known</u> Tommy, he <u>had</u> three different <u>jobs</u>.   **A B C D**
    A   B   C   D

20. She <u>hasn't</u> <u>washed</u> the dishes or <u>made</u> the beds <u>already</u>.   **A B C D**
        A   B   C   D

Test: Units 22–25

DIRECTIONS: Circle the letter of the correct answer to complete each sentence.

Example:

Jackie never _____ coffee.   A (B) C D
    (A) drink   (C) is drinking
    (B) drinks   (D) was drinking

1. I have _____ boss in the world.   A B C D
    (A) a good   (C) the best
    (B) best   (D) the better

2. Jessica is an excellent employee. She works   A B C D
   _____, and she's very dependable.
    (A) as hard   (C) harder than
    (B) hard   (D) hardly

3. The apple pie smells _____.   A B C D
    (A) more wonderfully   (C) wonderful
    (B) the most wonderfully   (D) wonderfully

4. The larger the apartment, the _____   A B C D
   the rent.
    (A) expensive   (C) more expensive
    (B) expensively   (D) most expensive

5. That's _____ story I have ever heard.   A B C D
    (A) a ridiculous   (C) the more ridiculous
    (B) the ridiculous   (D) the most ridiculous

6. This living room isn't as _____ ours.   A B C D
    (A) big as   (C) bigger than
    (B) bigger   (D) biggest

7. Stella drives more _____ Phil.   A B C D
    (A) careful as   (C) careful than
    (B) carefully as   (D) carefully than

8. Is there anything else on TV? This show doesn't seem _____.   A B C D
    (A) interested   (C) interestingly
    (B) interesting   (D) more interested

9. Riding in a car is more dangerous _____ flying.   A B C D
    (A) as   (C) than
    (B) from   (D) that

10. Please call if you're going to arrive _____.   A B C D
    (A) as late   (C) lately
    (B) late   (D) later than

11. It's getting more and _____ to find a cheap apartment.   A B C D
    (A) difficult   (C) more difficult
    (B) less difficult   (D) more difficult than

12. She plays the piano _____ as she sings.   A B C D
    (A) as beautiful   (C) more beautifully
    (B) as beautifully   (D) the most beautifully

PART TWO

DIRECTIONS: Each sentence has four underlined words or phrases. The four underlined parts of the sentence are marked A, B, C, and D. Circle the letter of the one underlined word or phrase that is NOT CORRECT.

Example:

Ana <u>rarely</u> <u>is drinking</u> coffee, but <u>this morning</u> she <u>is having</u> a cup.   A (B) C D
     A   B   C   D

13. Today will be <u>colder,</u> <u>wetter</u>, and <u>windier</u> <u>that</u> yesterday.   A B C D
                 A   B   C   D

14. This <u>nice</u> <u>new</u> apartment looks <u>perfectly</u> for a <u>young</u> couple.   A B C D
        A   B   C   D

15. Our <u>new</u> telephone answering machine doesn't operate as <u>quiet</u> <u>as</u>   A B C D
     A   B C
our <u>old</u> one.
     D

16. The clothes at Brooks are <u>nicer,</u> <u>interesting</u>, and <u>less expensive</u> <u>than</u>   A B C D
                          A   B   C   D
the clothes at B & S Department Store.

17. This is the <u>more interesting</u> and the <u>funniest</u> book I have <u>ever</u> <u>read</u>.   A B C D
           A   B   C   D

18. Thompson controlled the ball <u>the best</u>, kicked the ball <u>the farthest</u>,   **A B C D**

                                         A   B

and ran the <u>faster</u> <u>of</u> all the players.

                C   D

19. The critic was <u>amused</u> by the <u>funny</u> story line, but she found the   **A B C D**

                            A   B

acting <u>extremely</u> <u>unexcited</u>.

            C   D

20. It's getting <u>easy</u> and <u>easier</u> to find a <u>good</u> <u>inexpensive</u> color TV.   **A B C D**

                A   B   C   D

TEST: UNITS 26–31

DIRECTIONS: Circle the letter of the correct answer to complete each sentence.

Example:

Jackie never _____ coffee.　　　　　　　　**A Ⓑ C D**

    (A) drink　　　　　　　　　　(C) is drinking
    (B) drinks　　　　　　　　　　(D) was drinking

1. Do you enjoy _____?　　　　　　　　**A B C D**
    (A) swim　　　　　　　　　　(C) the swimming
    (B) swimming　　　　　　　　(D) to swim

2. I'm looking forward to _____ on vacation.　　　　　　　　**A B C D**
    (A) be going　　　　　　　　(C) going
    (B) go　　　　　　　　　　　(D) have gone

3. The doctor advised Mike to stop _____.　　　　　　　　**A B C D**
    (A) for smoking　　　　　　(C) smoking
    (B) smoke　　　　　　　　　(D) to smoke

4. She's going on a diet in order _____ weight.　　　　　　　　**A B C D**
    (A) for not gaining　　　　(C) not to gain
    (B) not for gaining　　　　(D) to gain not

5. I'm excited _____ starting my new job.　　　　　　　　**A B C D**
    (A) about　　　　　　　　　(C) of
    (B) for　　　　　　　　　　(D) to

6. Maria is not used to _____ alone.　　　　　　　　**A B C D**
    (A) live　　　　　　　　　　(C) lived
    (B) lives　　　　　　　　　(D) living

7. Have you ever considered _____ jobs?　　　　　　　　**A B C D**
    (A) change　　　　　　　　(C) changing
    (B) changed　　　　　　　　(D) to change

8. Where did he use to _____?   A B C D
  (A) live   (C) lives
  (B) lived   (D) living

9. Meng is interested _____ to college.   A B C D
  (A) for going   (C) to go
  (B) in going   (D) to going

PART TWO

DIRECTIONS: Each sentence has four underlined words or phrases. The four underlined parts of the sentence are marked A, B, C, and D. Circle the letter of the <u>one</u> underlined word or phrase that is NOT CORRECT.

Example:

Ana <u>rarely</u> <u>is drinking</u> coffee, but <u>this morning</u> she <u>is having</u> a cup.   A Ⓑ C D
     A   B   C   D

10. <u>Collecting</u> <u>stamps</u> <u>are</u> <u>a</u> popular hobby.   A B C D
        A   B   C D

11. Bo needs a ladder because he's <u>not</u> <u>enough tall</u> <u>to reach</u> the shelf.   A B C D
                            A   B   C D

12. When <u>do</u> you <u>expect</u> <u>him</u> <u>being</u> here?   A B C D
         A   B   C   D

13. <u>Before</u> <u>leaving</u> the office, please <u>remember</u> <u>locking</u> the door.   A B C D
     A   B   C   D

14. Fran <u>enjoys</u> <u>dancing</u> and looks forward <u>to</u> <u>learn</u> the latest dances.   A B C D
         A   B   C D

15. After <u>moving</u> to Canada, Monica had to get <u>used</u> <u>to</u> <u>do</u> everything   A B C D
       A   B C D
in English.

16. Sue was so excited <u>about</u> <u>winning</u> the contest that she <u>forgot</u>   A B C D
                         A   B   C
<u>meeting</u> her husband at the restaurant.
   D

17. Scott <u>didn't run</u> fast <u>enough</u> <u>for</u> <u>win</u> the race.   A B C D
         A   B   C D

18. Erica <u>avoids</u> <u>going</u> <u>to</u> parties because she has trouble <u>to remember</u>   A B C D
        A   B C   D
people's names.

19. <u>To do</u> sit-ups <u>is</u> hard work, and many people don't <u>enjoy</u> <u>doing</u> them.   A B C D
    A   B   C   D

20. Jimmy's father forced <u>him</u> <u>to apologize</u> <u>of</u> <u>breaking</u> the window.   A B C D
                      A   B   C   D

TEST: UNITS 32–36

DIRECTIONS: Circle the letter of the correct answer to complete each sentence.

Example:

Jackie never _____ coffee.   A (B) C D

    (A) drink   (C) is drinking
    (B) drinks   (D) was drinking

1. According to the law, everyone must   A B C D
_____ a license in order to drive.
    (A) has   (C) have to
    (B) have   (D) to have

2. _____ rain tomorrow?   A B C D
    (A) Is it going to   (C) Should it
    (B) May it   (D) Would it

3. I _____ arrive on time, so please start   A B C D
dinner without me.
    (A) could   (C) may not
    (B) may   (D) should

4. Jamie prefers working at home _____   A B C D
working in an office.
    (A) more   (C) that
    (B) than   (D) to

5. You _____ forget to pay your taxes.   A B C D
    (A) don't have to   (C) must
    (B) have to   (D) must not

6. According to the weather forecast, there   A B C D
_____ some rain tomorrow.
    (A) could   (C) may be
    (B) may   (D) maybe

7. It's dark out. It _____ be late.   A B C D
   (A) could   (C) must
   (B) might   (D) ought to

8. **A:** Is Doug an exchange student?   A B C D
   B: I'm not sure. He _____.
   (A) could   (C) must not be
   (B) couldn't   (D) could be

9. When _____ you supposed to call Matt?   A B C D
   (A) do   (C) must
   (B) are   (D) should

10. You _____ buy a gift, but you can if you want to.   A B C D
   (A) have to   (C) must
   (B) don't have to   (D) must not

11. **A:** _____ the package arrive tomorrow?   A B C D
   B: It might. I mailed it two days ago.
   (A) Could   (C) May
   (B) Do you prefer   (D) Must

12. **A:** Do you think Warren is over twenty?   A B C D
   B: He _____ be. I've known him for more than twenty
      years!
   (A) could   (C) might
   (B) has to   (D) must not

13. **A:** Are you going to the party tonight?   A B C D
   B: I _____. I'm pretty tired.
   (A) could   (C) 'd prefer to
   (B) don't like to   (D) might not

PART TWO

DIRECTIONS: Each sentence has four underlined words or phrases. The four underlined parts of the sentence are marked A, B, C, and D. Circle the letter of the <u>one</u> underlined word or phrase that is NOT CORRECT.

Example:

Ana <u>rarely</u> <u>is drinking</u> coffee, but <u>this morning</u> she <u>is having</u> a cup.   A (B) C D
    A   B   C   D

14. <u>I'd</u> rather <u>having</u> dinner at home <u>than</u> <u>eat</u> out.   A B C D
    A   B   C D

15. My sister <u>may</u> <u>arrives</u> before <u>I can</u> <u>get</u> to the train station.   A B C D
          A   B   C D

16. Why <u>do</u> you <u>prefer</u> newspapers <u>than</u> magazines<u>?</u>   **A   B   C   D**
       A   B   C   D

17. Jared <u>will be</u> <u>supposed</u> <u>to be</u> there tomorrow, but he <u>can't</u> go.   **A   B   C   D**
        A   B   C   D

18. It <u>must</u> rain <u>tonight</u>, so I <u>prefer</u> <u>to stay</u> home.   **A   B   C   D**
   A   B   C   D

19. You <u>don't have to</u> <u>drive</u> so fast or you <u>could</u> <u>get</u> a ticket.   **A   B   C   D**
           A   B   C   D

20. Everyone <u>have to</u> <u>come</u> on time unless <u>they'd rather</u> <u>miss</u> the   **A   B   C   D**
          A   B   C   D
opening speech.

TEST: UNITS 37–38

PART ONE

DIRECTIONS: *Circle the letter of the correct answer to complete each sentence. Use Ø when no word is needed.*

Example:

Jackie never _____ coffee.   A (B) C D

    (A) drink   (C) is drinking
    (B) drinks   (D) was drinking

1. _____ the mail arrived yet?   A B C D
    (A) Are   (C) Has
    (B) Is   (D) Have

2. She was unhappy because _____ of her   A B C D
friends sent her birthday cards.
    (A) a few   (C) few
    (B) a little   (D) little

3. They didn't have _____ shoes in my size.   A B C D
    (A) a great deal of   (C) much
    (B) a lot of   (D) some

4. Can you lend me _____ money?   A B C D
    (A) little   (C) many
    (B) some   (D) a few

5. _____ university is larger than a college.   A B C D
    (A) A   (C) The
    (B) An   (D) Ø

6. That's _____ best story I've ever heard.   A B C D
    (A) a   (C) the
    (B) an   (D) Ø

7. _____ music is Jane's favorite pastime.   A B C D
    (A) A   (C) The
    (B) An   (D) Ø

8. You have to protect your skin from   A   B   C   D
_____ sun.
(A) a   (C) the
(B) an   (D) Ø

9. Pauline doesn't eat _____ spaghetti.   A   B   C   D
(A) much   (C) the
(B) many   (D) a few

10. A: What does David do?   A   B   C   D
   B: He's _____ accountant.
(A) a   (C) the
(B) an   (D) Ø

11. Can you turn on _____ TV? I want to watch the news.   A   B   C   D
(A) a   (C) the
(B) an   (D) Ø

12. A: I rented _____ video last night.   A   B   C   D
   B: Oh? Which one?
(A) a   (C) the
(B) an   (D) Ø

PART TWO

*DIRECTIONS: Each sentence has four underlined words or phrases. The
four underlined parts of the sentence are marked A, B, C, and D. Circle
the letter of the <u>one</u> underlined word or phrase that is NOT CORRECT.*

Example:

Ana <u>rarely</u> <u>is drinking</u> coffee, but <u>this morning</u> she <u>is having</u> a cup.   A (B) C D
     A   B   C   D

13. <u>The</u> news <u>were</u> very sad, and everyone <u>was</u> talking about <u>it</u>.   A   B   C   D
    A   B   C   D

14. Jackie <u>has</u> been <u>a</u> honor student ever since she began her <u>studies</u> at   A   B   C   D
        A   B   C
<u>the university</u>.
    D

15. I need <u>some advice</u> about what to bring to my <u>aunt's</u> house on   A   B   C   D
         A   B
<u>thanksgiving</u> next <u>Thursday</u>.
    C   D

16. How <u>many</u> times do I have to tell you not to leave <u>your</u> wet <u>shoes</u>   A   B   C   D
      A   B   C
on <u>a</u> kitchen floor?
   D

17. Mathematics <u>are</u> Sally's favorite school <u>subject</u>, and she always <u>gets</u>   A   B   C   D
            A   B   C
high <u>grades</u>.
   D

18. I have <u>a little</u> money, so I can't take <u>a</u> vacation until <u>next</u> year at <u>the</u>   **A   B   C   D**
       A   B   C   D
<u>earliest</u>.

19. We need to pick up <u>some sugar</u> and <u>banana</u> at <u>the</u> supermarket on   **A   B   C   D**
                  A   B   C

<u>the</u> way home.
  D

20. Pat turned on <u>the</u> TV in order to see <u>the</u> weather report on <u>an</u>   **A   B   C   D**
             A   B   C

evening <u>news</u>.
    D

ANSWER KEY FOR TESTS

Note: Correct responses for Part Two questions appear in parentheses ( ).

ANSWER KEY FOR TEST:
UNITS 1–8

PART ONE
1. B
2. C
3. A
4. B
5. C
6. B
7. A
8. D
9. B
10. A
11. D
12. B
13. A
14. B
15. A
16. A
17. A
18. B
19. D
20. C
21. B
22. B
23. C
24. D
25. A
26. D
27. A
28. A
29. A
30. C
31. D
32. B
33. D
34. B
35. C
36. D

PART TWO
37. D (is taking OR is going to take)
38. D (wants)
39. D (like)
40. B (eats)
41. B (are you)
42. A (doesn't)
43. B (she rarely)
44. D (don't look)
45. A (always works)
46. D (feels)
47. C (is shining)
48. D (dropped)
49. A (was)
50. B (use to)
51. D (got)
52. C (got)
53. A (did you)
54. B (was driving)
55. A (gets)
56. D (will tell OR is going to tell)
57. C (I leave)
58. B (is going to be)
59. A (won't)
60. D (is going to have OR is having)

ANSWER KEY FOR TEST:
UNITS 9–10

PART ONE
1. B
2. B
3. D
4. A
5. B
6. D
7. C
8. B
9. D
10. A
11. D

PART TWO
12. A (it over)
13. D (me)
14. B (called)
15. D (you up)
16. C (yourself OR yourselves)
17. A (each other OR one another)
18. B (each other's)
19. D (myself)
20. D (pick up OR pick some stamps up)

ANSWER KEY FOR TEST:
UNITS 11–15

PART ONE
1.	A	7.	B
2.	B	8.	B
3.	D	9.	C
4.	D	10.	B
5.	C	11.	A
6.	C	12.	A

PART TWO
13. A (will you)
14. D (?)
15. C (if)
16. C (have)
17. B (leave)
18. D (*please* goes after *you, remember,* or *newspaper*)
19. A (to be)
20. B (telling)

ANSWER KEY FOR TEST:
UNITS 16–21

PART ONE
1.	B	8.	C
2.	B	9.	C
3.	D	10.	D
4.	B	11.	B
5.	D	12.	B
6.	C	13.	B
7.	D	14.	D

PART TWO
15.	C (worked)	18.	D (got)
16.	A (has)	19.	C (has had)
17.	A (rented)	20.	D (yet)

ANSWER KEY FOR TEST:
UNITS 22–25

PART ONE
1.	C	7.	D
2.	B	8.	B
3.	C	9.	C
4.	C	10.	B
5.	D	11.	C
6.	A	12.	B

PART TWO
13.	D (than)	17.	A (most interesting)
14.	C (perfect)	18.	C (fastest)
15.	B (quietly)	19.	D (unexciting)
16.	B (more interesting)	20.	A (easier)

ANSWER KEY FOR TEST:
UNITS 26–31

PART ONE
1.	B	6.	D
2.	C	7.	C
3.	C	8.	A
4.	C	9.	B
5.	A		

PART TWO
10.	C (is)	16.	D (to meet)
11.	B (tall enough)	17.	C (to)
12.	D (to be)	18.	D (remembering)
13.	D (to lock)	19.	A (Doing)
14.	D (learning)	20.	C (for)
15.	D (doing)		

ANSWER KEY FOR TEST:
UNITS 32–36

PART ONE
1.	B	8.	D
2.	A	9.	B
3.	C	10.	B
4.	D	11.	A
5.	D	12.	B
6.	C	13.	D
7.	C		

PART TWO
14.	B (have)	18.	A (might OR could)
15.	B (arrive)	19.	A (must not OR 'd better not)
16.	C (to)	20.	A (has to)
17.	A (is OR was)		

ANSWER KEY FOR TEST:
UNITS 37–38

PART ONE
1.	C	7.	D
2.	C	8.	C
3.	B	9.	A
4.	B	10.	B
5.	A	11.	C
6.	C	12.	A

PART TWO
13.	B (was)	17.	A (is)
14.	B (an)	18.	A (little)
15.	C (Thanksgiving)	19.	B (bananas)
16.	D (the)	20.	C (the)